a journey to FINANCIAL FREEDOM

Transforming a marketable skill into financial independence

DANCHO DIMKOV

First published in 2024

© Copyright Dancho Dimkov

All rights reserved. No part of this publication may be reproduced, stored in or introduced into a retrieval system, or transmitted, in any form, or by any means (electronic, mechanical, photocopying, recording or otherwise) without the prior written permission of the publisher.

The right of Dancho Dimkov to be identified as the author of this work has been asserted by him in accordance with the Copyright, Designs and Patents Act 1988.

This book is sold subject to the condition that it shall not, by way of trade or otherwise, be lent, resold, hired out, or otherwise circulated without the publisher's prior consent in any form of binding or cover other than that in which it is published and without a similar condition including this condition being imposed on the subsequent purchaser.

Cover design by Martin Kovachki

Illustrations by Martin Kovachki

Table of Contents

Introduction 1

PART I: 7

The Inception Of A Book 7

1. Develop A Skill **19**

How I started my journey 21

Be flexible 24

Learn from the greats..27

Not sure where to start? 29

Choose any skill 32

What if I am bad at that skill now? 36

Key takeaways 39

2. Start Freelancing **41**

You don't need to quit your job............................47

Freelance sales funnel 51

Your freelance KPIs...54

A full-time freelancer 59

Cost-benefit analysis..61

Key takeaways 67

3. Become An Entrepreneur...........................**69**

Beyond freelancing..70

My entrepreneurial vision.....................................73

A taste of being a leader 76

Scaling the freelance pool......................................82

Recruiting the right team 83

Key takeaways 90

PART II: **91**

4. Register A Startup **93**

Look at the worst-case scenario 95

Plan vs. reality 105

The call that changed everything 110

The problem 116

Key takeaways 119

5. Grow Your Business **121**

Delegate. Delegate. Delegate 126

Standardise your business 134

Invest in marketing and sales 137

Strategic decisions for growth 141

Decision #1: Specialised service 142

Decision #2: Specialised target 147

Decision #3: Pre-packaged solutions 150

Decision #4: Increased prices 154

Key takeaways 156

6. Evolve Into A Consultant **159**

Craft a consulting framework 163

Network 167

Building a local network 168

Building an international network 170

Become a thought leader 172

Publish a book 175

Launch an academy 179

Become a keynote speaker 182

Crafting your consulting services 187

The synergy...192

Key takeaways 195

PART III: **197**

7. What Is Financial Freedom For You? **199**

How much do you actually need? 205

How much you spend affects how much you need.........206

Where you live affects how much you need 208

How much do you want to spend?.......................209

The formula for passive income 210

Key takeaways 214

8. How To Get There?... **215**

Strategy #1: Grow and sell my agency business..............216

Strategy #2: Double down on digital products.................219

Strategy #3: Personal strategies for financial freedom 225

Strategy #4: Grow my business into a passive salary 235

Strategy #5: Mixing the strategies 242

Key takeaways 244

Done. Now What?.. **245**

Acknowledgments **249**

The Author **251**

INTRODUCTION

Have you ever imagined a life where money doesn't limit your choices? A life where you're not just surviving but thriving, free from the constraints of a nine-to-five job, living each day on your own terms. This is not just a dream; it's a possibility – a reality that can be achieved through the entrepreneurial journey I'm about to share with you.

You might be a recent graduate with a head full of ideas but uncertain about the first steps to take. Perhaps you're a mid-career professional, feeling stuck in the routine grind, dreaming of breaking free and starting something of your own. Or maybe you're a seasoned freelancer or a small business owner, looking for ways to scale your operations and elevate your financial status.

Perhaps you're scared – I've been scared too – but you can ground yourself with a simple question: "What's the worst that can happen?"

I will take you through my personal journey – an odyssey that started with nothing more than a skill and a vision. I

A journey to financial freedom

have shared my insights, struggles, and triumphs to inspire, guide, and motivate you to embark on your own path to financial freedom.

I started as a one-man band alongside a day job, then worked with a team of freelancers. Then I hired my wife before founding my company with four interns in 2016. Less than a year later I had 25-plus employees. I grew my business, evolved into consultancy and recently stepped away from day-to-day operations to spend more time with my family, aged under 40.

It's a journey that many would say is reserved for the fortunate few. But here's the truth I've discovered: financial freedom isn't about luck; it's about making informed choices, strategic planning, and, most importantly, having the courage to take that first step into the unknown.

A moment of clarity washed over me as I sat in the bustling airport in my home city of Skopje, Macedonia. I realised that the lessons I had learned, the battles I had fought, and the victories I had savoured could light the way for others on their path to financial freedom. I understood that my entrepreneurial journey, with all its ups and downs, could offer hope, direction, and practical guidance to those who dared to dream of a life ruled not by financial limitations but by personal aspirations.

This book is my invitation to you to step off the beaten path and explore the possibilities that await when you dare

Introduction

to pursue financial freedom. It's an exploration of what it means to transform a skill, a simple, everyday ability (anything you can learn to do that others will pay for) into a thriving business that doesn't just sustain but empowers you to live the life you've always imagined.

You'll find yourself on a journey with me from the sleepless nights filled with doubts to the exhilarating highs of breakthroughs, from the initial tentative steps of a novice entrepreneur to the confident strides of a business owner basking in the freedom of financial independence.

What does "financial freedom" really mean? It's a term often tossed around in conversations about wealth and success, but its true essence goes far deeper than just having a lot of money. Financial freedom is a multifaceted concept, a state of being that transcends the mere accumulation of wealth. It's the liberation from financial constraints, the ability to make choices that align with your deepest desires and values, not just your economic necessities.

To me, financial freedom is not just about accumulating wealth; it's about having the choice and the ability to live life on your terms. It's the liberty to make decisions based not on financial constraints but on passion, interest, and fulfilment. Financial freedom is about embracing a life where your time is truly yours.

A journey to financial freedom

At its heart, financial freedom is about control – control over your time, your choices, and your future. It's about the ability to make life decisions without being overly stressed about the financial impact because you are prepared. You have the resources, the cushion, the financial backup to support those choices. It's not necessarily about living a lavish lifestyle or having a hefty bank balance; it's about having your finances aligned in such a way that they enable, not restrict, your life's choices and aspirations.

To me, financial freedom meant the ability to pursue my entrepreneurial dreams without the crippling fear of financial ruin. It meant the opportunity to experiment, to take calculated risks, and to embrace new ventures, knowing that my financial foundation was solid. It was about creating a life where work became a choice, a joy, rather than an obligatory means to an end.

Financial freedom also brings with it a sense of security and peace of mind. It's about knowing that you and your loved ones are secure, that your financial future is stable, and that you have the means to weather life's unexpected turns. It's the peace that comes from knowing you're not just one paycheck away from turmoil, the comfort of having a safety net that allows you to sleep soundly at night.

The purpose of this book is twofold: to demystify the journey to financial freedom and to offer you a companion on your path to achieving it.

Introduction

This book, "A Journey to Financial Freedom" is a chronicle of my journey – from picking up a marketable skill (you can substitute any skill or passion of your own) to becoming financially independent. But more than that, it's a guide to your potential.

I have shared my real, lived perspective on achieving financial freedom. Unlike many resources that offer theoretical advice or unattainable success stories, this book is grounded in practicality and relatability. It's about real struggles, real strategies, and real success. It's not just a showcase of where I've been; it's a guidebook for where you can go: a roadmap, not just a destination, and one which offers you actionable insights and strategies.

Whether you're a budding entrepreneur, a freelancer looking to expand, or a professional seeking a significant change, this book is for you. It's for anyone who dreams of a life defined by freedom, for anyone who wants to transform their passion into a livelihood. This book is a testament to the fact that with the right approach, dedication, and mindset, achieving financial independence is not just a far-off dream.

Through the pages of this book, you'll gain insights into the journey from developing a simple skill to building a business that provides not just financial stability but also freedom. You'll learn about the highs and lows of entrepreneurship, the challenges of starting a business, and the triumphs of seeing it succeed.

A journey to financial freedom

You'll discover strategies for growing your skill set, expanding your business, and ultimately, paving your path to financial freedom. These are not just theories; they are practical, real-world experiences and lessons that I have lived and learned.

This book is more than a mere collection of words and pages. It's a compass, a guide to navigate out of the financial maze that traps so many. It's a story, but also a strategy.

It's my story, but it could be yours. So here it is.

PART I:

THE PATH TO SUCCESS

THE INCEPTION OF A BOOK

"This is your boarding announcement for Flight W67765 to Malta. All passengers are requested to proceed to the gate area." I could hear the speaker at the Macedonian airport calling us to board. It was mid-October 2022, and the weather was perfect for a new adventure.

I was going on a holiday with my family – my wife Maja, who was seven months pregnant, and my five-year-old son, Metodija. It was our third family holiday that year.

A journey to financial freedom

We'd already been to Egypt and the United States. Bringing up a child requires a lot of commitment in parallel with work – and we were soon to be blessed with another.

From a business aspect, I had an upcoming summit, a keynote speaking gig in Albania, an entrepreneurship workshop in Armenia, and a strategic workshop in Macedonia. A typical schedule for a busy entrepreneur who wants to scale their business internationally.

While waiting to board, I noticed my son Metodija playing superheroes all by himself. I went to join him. I had two hours ahead of me to think and stress, why not play now?

If you have kids, you know how easily they get bored. After less than 15 minutes of playing in the imaginary arena, Metodija decided he's not into that any longer.

So here I was, left to my anxious thoughts again. On the one hand, I was still deeply involved in my business operationally. I struggled to create a system that could operate without me as I had too much on my plate. On the other hand, as a side project, I committed to write a chapter for an upcoming collaboration book.

***

"This is the final boarding call for flight W67765 to Malta."

The lady on the speaker interrupted my thoughts, and we got in the queue. Metodija was jumping around while my

The inception of a book

wife was trying to keep things under control. I am still amazed at how she handles two kids (me and Metodija), and she was ready for a third one. She is a superhero.

As we entered the plane, I had to make sure Maja and Metodija were comfortable. I tried entertaining Metodija again, but he was already tired and wanted to sleep next to his mummy. This gave me the opportunity to continue with my thoughts during the flight.

I had to make a decision. I have already agreed to write a chapter of a new book about leadership with seven other entrepreneurs, and I needed a topic. Something I could write around 3,000–4,000 words about.

My thoughts ran to the call I had with the publisher just yesterday. What should I be writing about in my chapter? As I wanted to use the book to position myself as a business expert, which topic would provide the best credibility for me?

A hard decision. I could write about so many topics, but I had only one chapter.

I could write about my extensive freelance experience, as I was 15-plus years in the freelance world with $400K+ in income on UpWork alone.

I could write about my broad entrepreneurship experience. My MSc degree in Entrepreneurship and the several entrepreneurial ventures under my belt would help me there.

A journey to financial freedom

I could write about growing SMEs. As an owner of BizzBee Solutions, I've worked with 500+ SMEs from around the world, helping them grow their businesses. I even did my Executive MBA degree in Management.

I could write about becoming a consultant. I started my DanchoDimkov.com brand and it was a success. Also, as I was involved in MCA2000 (Management Consulting Association) in Macedonia, I had a lot to share.

I could also write about the ultimate entrepreneurial goal – financial freedom. In the last few years, I've put a significant effort into making BizzBee sellable as a business, as well as exploring diversification in financial strategies – real estate, stocks, investment funds, crypto, etc.

So, I was at a crossroads. Choosing a topic for a book chapter feels permanent. And I wanted it to be about something I want to be known for.

While listening to one of the podcasts I have queued up for today's flight, I remembered the publisher's words over the phone – "Why don't you write about all of them? Why don't you cover your journey – from how you started to where you are now?"

That is a good idea, I initially thought. I can create a chapter covering the journey from a skill to financial freedom.

As I was outlining the seven stages of my journey, I smiled. Each of them can easily be a separate chapter in a

The inception of a book

new book. A book where I can share my experience and business insights.

But I couldn't. A thought rushed through my brain. My first book took me two years to write and publish. It was a headache writing a book and running a business. *Sweet Leads* was published in the UK, and it was a book that I poured my heart and soul into.

And I intended to make *Sweet Leads* the first part of a trilogy. It covers the science and art of reaching out to cold prospects, engaging them, building meaningful relationships, and bringing them to a scheduled meeting. The other, *Sweet Deals* and *Sweet Growth*, are about how to get and keep clients. The books and everything around them are a three-to-five-year plan for growing my business. So, I had enough on my plate.

"Please fasten your seatbelts as we are approaching landing."

Wow, have one-and-a-half hours passed already? I look around; Metodija is watching cartoons on the phone, and Maja is gazing out of the window, enjoying the view over the sea and the coastline. I really hope she had a peaceful trip.

For a second, I forgot about the pending chapter and continued exploring the idea of writing a whole book about my entrepreneurial journey. Do I have the time to commit to a new project?

A journey to financial freedom

Boom. Reality hit hard. Will I be able to squeeze in a book with the baby two months away?

Isn't it easier to do 2,000–3,000 words on a more specific topic and get on with the collaboration project? After all, I have committed only to a chapter, not a whole new book and a chapter.

But then I had a light-bulb moment. This book is not like *Sweet Leads*. It took me two years to publish *Sweet Leads* because it is a framework book on B2B prospecting and outreach.

As such, it required insights from all our clients, creating and optimising frameworks, creating processes and flows – and then ensuring any business can apply them. In addition, it required a lot of additional work in standardisation of the methods and researching our BizzBee Solutions history to find suitable client examples.

A Journey to Financial Freedom is something different. All I need to write this book is enough time to reflect and document the stages I was going through while growing BizzBee Solutions and the struggles at each stage.

It will describe my personal journey – I don't need empirical data and extensive research. It is what happened to me and how I dealt with certain situations.

"Cabin crew, please prepare for landing."

I smiled again.

The inception of a book

I am on a week-long holiday in Malta before I return to the business jungle. What if I use this one week to do this book project? What if I dedicate 2–3 hours daily and work on the book?

Worst case scenario, I will make it a chapter. But what if I manage to actually write it? A brand-new book?! Wouldn't it be amazing?

"I need 2–3 hours a day for a week. This week, while we're in Malta," I said to Maja, without any context.

"For what?" as she had no idea what I had in my mind.

"I am considering writing a new book," I replied.

"But why?" Maja asked, a bit confused.

That was a really hard question. Really, why should I bother? Why don't I enjoy my vacation and lay on the beach all day long?

"To help anyone at the beginning of their career who consider taking a route on their own. Or at least show them one path to financial freedom that they can follow, pointing out all the difficulties and joys at each stage."

"I wish someone had done this for me. I wish I had someone to give me a roadmap, a journey that, if I liked, I could follow."

Most of the books for financial freedom out there are for employees. How to save on your salary and invest the savings towards retiring early. But what if you don't have a

A journey to financial freedom

salary? I haven't seen a book focused on entrepreneurs and business owners – and how they can achieve financial freedom.

When I look at my journey now, it is pretty easy to write about the past, reflecting on what had already happened. Back then, I was struggling to make the right choices.

But now, after more than a decade of experience, I can look back and draw a roadmap anyone can follow to succeed. And I can help them avoid the most common pitfalls and mistakes. That I can do.

"That is a great idea. I would love to see what you come up with. Do it," Maja said with a smile.

I don't think she was fully aware of what we were getting ourselves into, but neither was I. All I knew was that I wanted to do this. And I was glad that my wife was here to support me.

And the plane landed.

In 90 minutes I had grown a chapter idea into an idea for a full book.

As we landed in Malta, our friend Vesna greeted us. Zlatko was at work. We were staying at Zlatko and Vesna's house. We talked, got several Cisk Lagers – the best Maltese beers – and settled in.

The inception of a book

So here is my commitment. I am on Day 1 in Malta. Maja and Metodija are already sleeping. Vesna is watching TV, and Zlatko is at work.

I thought it was the perfect time to write the introduction for this book.

For the next seven days I will try to spend the best time with my family and friends, which is why I came to Malta after all. It is my third visit, and I know all the hidden gems that Malta can offer.

And I will also try to find a couple of hours in the day to work on this book. And that means sitting in a quiet place, thinking about my journey, and actually writing about it.

So, the current goal is to spend seven days in Malta and use each day to create a seven-chapter book. And have fun, too.

***

"Are you still up?" It was Zlatko coming back from work at 1:30am. I was deep into writing.

"Yep, I was waiting for you to come back from work," I hugged him. I had so much more to write.

But I closed the laptop and hugged my friend, whom I had known since kindergarten, practically my whole life.

It's been a long day. I will continue writing tomorrow.

1. Develop A Skill

Sunday morning. Shops are closed in Malta, so there isn't much to do.

I woke up quite exhausted from last night's writing marathon, but with my heart full of joy.

We scrambled some eggs for breakfast – I make the perfect scrambled eggs – and before you knew it, we were off to the beach.

I forgot how much I have missed Malta. The hot weather, the smell of mist in the air, the sound of the waves and

A journey to financial freedom

the crowded streets. It's been three years since I last came here, but it felt like forever.

And I love Sundays. It is a calm day, and I usually spend Sundays with my family. Monday to Friday is quite crazy at work and, unfortunately, I occasionally work some Saturdays. But never Sundays. That is the time dedicated to family.

At the beach, I had an interesting conversation with Zlatko. He was a full-time employee, but wanted to start something additional on the side. Something that can bring some extra income. Should he pursue a mixologist side gig and become even better at mixing cocktails? Or perhaps become a beer maker, brewing beer. He had a few other alternatives and was not sure which one was most "profitable".

My answer was simple. It doesn't matter, choose one and start learning about it. You can always change your mind along the way. And that conversation was my inspiration for the first chapter of the book.

After the beach, I got back to my room and opened my laptop. I was ready for the first chapter. Zlatko had to go to work, his wife was still at work, and Maja was preparing a festive lunch. I could smell the fresh baked potatoes and carrots with chicken fillet.

Perfect time for me to get the ball rolling.

Develop a skill

I want to use this first chapter to quash a myth. I want to shatter the belief that you need to be an expert in a field to be able to offer a service. Like, everyone was born expert? Of course not.

HOW I STARTED MY JOURNEY

Back in 2008, I was in my third year at university. Like most twentysomethings, all I thought about was parties and drinking. I don't regret it at all. I had a youth and experiences worth remembering.

My school system was brilliant – I did a lot of partying and enjoying life for three weeks each month. Then exam week came along, and I would lock myself in the study room for one week. It worked for me, as I got good grades, my parents were pleased and kept paying for my education in the capital, and my teachers were happy.

But unfortunately, there were also assignments. I found them a distraction and, of course, didn't like them. However, I was not aware that a single assignment could change the course of my life.

For one project, I had to study mobile marketing. While researching the topic, I realised that we didn't have mobile marketing in Macedonia or the Balkans. It was 2008, so there was no Facebook or any other social media platform.

A journey to financial freedom

That project assignment inspired me to start my first business, AdvertSMS. I was 21 years old and officially an entrepreneur.

I had zero business knowledge and no experience. The chance of succeeding was worse than gambling. I borrowed €1,500 from a bank and €500 from my brother. My brother said I could pay him back when I could, and the bank gave me €50 instalments for three years. So, I started AdvertSMS with €2,000 in total. Quite scary for a 21-year-old. The money I got lasted for a few months. Then I had to become creative in running a business without any money.

I really wouldn't recommend starting a business without any business knowledge and experience. I think that is how most entrepreneurs start. And it is why nine out of ten startups fail.

And so did mine.

But I don't see it as a failure. I learned a lot from it. At least common business knowledge – creating invoices, making sales calls, and talking to businesses. I also learned from my mistakes. I now realise that if I have worked for another company for a few months – I could have avoided most of the mistakes. It is much cheaper to learn while being paid for it. I think the main reason why my first business failed was because I didn't look at the market needs. Instead, I looked at an interesting business idea

Develop a skill

that I want to pursue. Typical rookie mistake, but it was quite painful.

Now that my first entrepreneurial journey was over, I had to get a job. It was within an international organisation (SNV – Netherlands Development Organisation). They noticed my entrepreneurial spirit and wanted to focus my business skills on agriculture, helping farmers and cooperatives grow their businesses.

I spent three years in that organisation and learned much about projects, programs, budgets, stakeholders, processes, and systems. I worked with multiple stakeholders, looking at problems from different points of view. Unfortunately, the organisation closed its offices in Macedonia, so I had to continue with my journey.

I found my next job at a UK software and hardware development company. I helped them establish their business presence in Macedonia from scratch. Establishing the formal business, finding a location, recruitment, and managing a development team. It took me three years to grow them into a 12-people team.

And in those three years, I was involved in many tech and "translation" activities. First, I translated business needs to developers, then translated developers' responses to the business people. But also, I learned how to grow and manage teams: a skill that you must have if you want to grow your own business. I left this company to pursue my freelance dream.

As you can see, the start of my career path was all over the place. I really believe this was a benefit – exploring and experiencing different industries gave me some broad experience and skill sets. And above all, I learned it is OK to change course.

BE FLEXIBLE

Instead of focusing on one thing and being great at it, I was driven by opportunities in the market. From entrepreneur to agriculture to software development. I wish I could have a career path from the beginning that I can follow. And it is a great advice for any employee.

Oh, I'm getting away from the subject. This isn't a book about finding a great job. Sorry if I disappointed you. The book is about how to grow to financial independence. Not how to get a better salary.

So, let's do a quick exercise. Imagine you have a million in your bank account. Congratulations! Now what? Being a millionaire:

What would you like to do?

What motivates and excites you?

What would you do for free?

This can be your career. However, in most cases, this is not your career path. Sorry, but I must be honest with

Develop a skill

you. Not many people get to do their dream job for a living. And each person's dream job evolves over time.

When you were five, you probably dreamed about being something completely different than you want to be now.

At 20–25 years old, did you still want the same job? Has it changed? And in most cases, people evolve into liking another profession and choosing a different career. Or the career chooses them.

But then, if I asked you at 40–45 years old if you still wanted the same career as you wanted at 25, would you keep the same path or change direction?

So, the ultimate question is – can you plan these things?

Well, you can't. Sorry if I burst your bubble. You can follow a certain career path for a while. But in most cases, life happens. You grow up and so do your dreams, hopes, and desires. So, you'll switch lanes. You have to be flexible and open to the idea that you might want to change your career.

And there is nothing wrong with that. We are humans; flexibility is in our nature. Take it from me – I had quite a few career changes, each with an ambitious career path.

At 21, I started a marketing agency – in the first few months, I was so excited about the marketing world that I decided I would build a career in marketing. I was wrong.

A journey to financial freedom

At 22, I was a business adviser in agriculture – again, I was excited. I even started looking at a master's degree in agriculture. That was that – I would specialise in business in agriculture. Wrong again.

At 25, I was establishing a software and hardware company in Macedonia. What an exciting career. And not to forget, a well-paid job. Considering it as a lifetime path, I did my executive MBA in agile software development methodologies. But, you've guessed it, I was wrong again.

At 29, I started BizzBee Solutions as a management consulting company. That was what I would do for the rest of my life. And I got the Certified Management Consultant (CMC) certification, joined a management consulting association, and started daydreaming about being the best consultant out there. Sounds dreamy, right?

Well, it wasn't.

At 33, I refocused BizzBee from consulting to an appointment-setting agency, specialising in the B2B segment for high-ticket service providers. I thought I would want to run this specialised agency for the rest of my life. And I started getting deep into sales. I was wrong.

Before 40, I genuinely hope to be retired, as all these changes are giving me a headache. However, I know I am on the right path to get there, and I am flexible enough to get feedback from the world and adjust accordingly.

Develop a skill

It is important to remember that flexibility in career paths is not only normal but often advantageous. The same principle applies here: you don't have to have it all figured out from the start to succeed. In fact, being open to change can be your greatest asset in navigating the winding road to financial independence.

LEARN FROM THE GREATS

If you're still sceptical about the power of career flexibility, let's look at some extraordinary individuals who embody this principle.

You know Elon Musk, right? He is a modern-day polymath who epitomises career flexibility. He co-founded Zip2, an online business directory and map service, which was sold to Compaq for nearly €300 million in 1999. Rather than sticking to the internet business, Musk moved on to X.com, an online payment company that eventually became PayPal after a merger, and was sold to eBay for €1.5 billion in stock.

Did he stop there? Not even close. Musk then shifted his focus entirely and founded SpaceX with the ambitious goal of reducing space transportation costs to make the colonisation of Mars possible. Parallel to SpaceX, he joined Tesla Motors, Inc. (now Tesla, Inc.) as chairman of the board and then CEO, taking on the auto industry with electric vehicles. But his ambitions don't stop there. He has initiated projects in solar energy through SolarCity,

A journey to financial freedom

neurotechnology through Neuralink, and even plans for a hyperloop transport system.

Elon Musk shows that not only is it OK to change career directions, but it can also be immensely rewarding. Each of his ventures was a gamble with high stakes and higher barriers to entry. Yet, his willingness to be flexible, to learn, and to adapt to completely new industries has made him one of the most impactful entrepreneurs of our time.

Another example is Jeff Bezos, the founder of Amazon. He started his career in the finance sector. He was vice-president of an investment bank before he decided to leave it all behind for the untamed world of online retail in the mid-90s. Amazon was initially a simple online bookstore. However, seeing the limitless potential of e-commerce, Bezos didn't keep Amazon one-dimensional. He expanded the company into selling everything from clothing to electronics and even groceries.

Bezos didn't stop at retail, either. Amazon Web Services (AWS), a subsidiary of Amazon providing on-demand cloud computing platforms, is a game-changer in the realm of cloud computing. The creation of Kindle revolutionised reading, and the acquisition of Whole Foods marked Amazon's foray into brick-and-mortar retail.

Under Bezos, Amazon has also ventured into media through Amazon Studios and has its eyes on space exploration through his other company, Blue Origin. Bezos demonstrates how sticking to one career or industry could

Develop a skill

limit one's growth potential. His ability to adapt, innovate, and venture into new avenues turned him into the world's richest man for several years.

And it is not only big names like Musk and Bezos that were flexible in their career journey. Take a look at your closer circle of family and friends. How many people do you know that started a career in one direction, thinking that it is their path, only to change direction after a few years? You can do it too.

NOT SURE WHERE TO START?

Choose something you like doing – even if you are not good at it.

I know most career consultants are trying to make you think five, ten or fifteen years in advance. And if you are certain that you know what you want, you win the jackpot. But most of us entrepreneurs are just one opportunity away from switching focus.

Most of the people I am talking to have trouble figuring out their business idea, something that they can grow into a business.

Is it really that hard to get a business idea?

I have more than ten business ideas every month, and I struggle to choose the right one.

A journey to financial freedom

So my focus is not on business idea generation. It is more on business idea evaluation and qualification.

We entrepreneurs are different because we see better than others. We can see business opportunities when ordinary people see nothing. If you are an entrepreneur, I know you have plenty of ideas. But it can be crippling not knowing which path to take. And that's why I want to introduce you to the term *Analysis Paralysis*.

Analysis Paralysis is the inability to make a decision because of too much information and overthinking a problem. If you find yourself stuck in this loop, you're not alone. Here are three practical strategies to break free and take that all-important first step:

Strategy 1: The Pareto Principle

Also known as the 80/20 rule[1], the Pareto Principle suggests that 80% of effects come from 20% of causes. In the context of decision-making, this means that a thorough analysis might not significantly outperform a quick yet informed decision. Apply this principle to quickly weed out ideas or options that are less likely to yield results, focusing your energies on those that promise the most impact.

---

[1] Davis, H. T., & Feldstein, M. L. (1979). The generalized Pareto law as a model for progressively censored survival data. Biometrika, 66(2), 299–306. https://doi.org/10.1093/biomet/66.2.299

Develop a skill

Strategy 2: Time-boxing

Set a specific time limit to make a decision. When the time is up, go with the best option you have at that moment. The simple act of setting a deadline can often sharpen your focus and expedite the decision-making process.

Strategy 3: The Two-Route approach

The first route is making an educated decision after in-depth planning and research. This is effective but time-consuming. The second route is the agile approach: make a choice based on the best information available, act on it, and pivot as necessary. Each approach has its merits, and the best one for you will depend on your unique circumstances and the stakes involved.

And that is the lesson of this chapter.

In the world of entrepreneurship and personal growth, the perfect decision is often elusive. What is attainable, however, is making a decision that's good enough for now and has the potential to become great through learning and adaptation. The key is to make a choice, take the first step, and be willing to pivot as you go along. Your path to financial independence doesn't have to be a straight line; it's the twists and turns that bring the most valuable lessons.

A journey to financial freedom

Choose any skill

Let me repeat myself. Just choose a skill. Any skill. And go with it.

I'll tell you a secret that I don't think I've shared before.

In high school, I was predetermined to become a software developer. I was spending too much time on my computer, I was proficient in several programming languages, and my brother was already enrolled in tech school.

Guess what? I joined the faculty of economics. My mother, father, and everyone around me were baffled. What do I know about economics? None of my close family was an entrepreneur, or had started a business.

My secret? I had two main reasons for studying economics.

The first reason was, well, perhaps not so noble. The student demographic for economics major comprised close to 90% of women. For a 19-year-old guy like me that was reason enough to choose economics.

The second justification was an assumption. As a maths and tech nerd, I would just have blended into tech school, surrounding myself with people like me. In exposing myself to economics, I got to learn stuff that I am not good at rather than just getting better at the things I'm already good at.

Develop a skill

Choosing economics over tech might have seemed counterintuitive at the time, but it paid dividends down the line when I decided to venture into entrepreneurship. While technical skills are undoubtedly valuable, my education in economics provided me with a different way of thinking. It provided me with a foundational business knowledge that I would have otherwise lacked. I understood market dynamics, consumer behaviour, and basic financial principles – all crucial for running a business. Had I gone down the tech route, I might have been technically proficient but wholly unprepared for the intricate dance of entrepreneurship.

It's a lesson in how sometimes the path less obvious can yield unexpected, yet essential, benefits for your future. Choose a skill you are good at and something you enjoy doing, but be open to the fact that you might no longer want this in the future, or the market might steer you differently.

Also, choose a skill you enjoy, as if you need to spend 12–18 hours per day developing it, at least you will enjoy those hours.

For me, that skill was entrepreneurship. I was helping excited entrepreneurs determine their market, competition, and business model. I was also helping tech entrepreneurs with soft skills to fine-tune their business ideas.

So, as an economist, I took the most straightforward route – offering business services.

A journey to financial freedom

But this book is about helping you make the right choice. If you know that you can pick any skill, knowing that you can change your mind at any point, does that make it an easier pick?

If so, pick now. Right now. And worry not. It will most probably change, but the beauty of life and entrepreneurship is in its impermanence.

Even if your first choice doesn't pan out as you'd hoped, you're still moving forward, gaining experiences and insights that you wouldn't have had otherwise. Remember, the cost of being wrong is far less than the cost of doing nothing. So, make that choice now. Your future self will thank you for having the courage to take that first step, even if it leads you somewhere entirely unexpected.

But you can afford to take a route, be wrong, and try another one. What's important here is that you'll undertake the second route with far more experience.

So, if you are a developer (or a wannabe developer), try to make it in that world.

If you are a digital marketer (or wannabe), what is the worst that can happen if you pursue a career in digital marketing?

So, how do you go about choosing a skill, especially when you're faced with an abundance of options? Here's a practical guide:

Develop a skill

1. **Identify your interests:** Make a list of things you're passionate about. It's easier to become proficient at something you enjoy.
2. **Evaluate market demand:** Research to see if there's a market for the skill you're interested in. No point in mastering something no one will pay for.
3. **Self-assessment:** Be brutally honest with yourself. Do you have a foundational understanding or talent in this area, or are you willing to put in the effort to develop it from scratch?
4. **Seek mentorship:** If possible, find someone already successful in the field and ask for their advice or mentorship.
5. **Trial period:** Dedicate a set period – say, three months – to intensely focus on this skill. Assess your enjoyment and aptitude as you go along.
6. **Be open to pivoting:** As you progress, keep in mind that it's okay to change course. Remember that flexibility can often be an asset, not a liability.
7. **Skill up and network:** As you grow more confident, start taking on small projects to build a portfolio. And don't forget to network within the industry; sometimes opportunities come from the most unexpected places.

By systematically going through these steps, you're not just aimlessly picking a skill but making an informed decision that aligns with both your personal interests and market demand. Remember, the skill you choose today doesn't have to be the one you stick with forever. As you evolve, your skill set should too.

WHAT IF I AM BAD AT THAT SKILL NOW?

Just as I mentioned earlier about being flexible and choosing any skill, it's equally crucial to remember that being bad at the outset is a part of the journey.

You're mistaken if you think this feeling is only at the beginning. It will last. Get used to it. I suck at many things that I am supposed to do now. I am confident that I will be terrible at any new activities I do for the first time.

It's okay to suck at something new. In fact, it's expected. Take me, for example. I committed to learning guitar in 2021. After six months, I could play a couple of chords. Not a concert performance, but progress, nonetheless. And it felt fantastic. Similarly, my Arabic lessons in 2022 started rough, but each failed sentence was a lesson in itself. Learning a new skill is all about embracing discomfort and failure.

Develop a skill

And this brings us full circle to the earlier points about being flexible and choosing any skill. You have to start somewhere, and it's okay if that start is less than perfect.

So if there is one lesson I can teach you, it is to get used to being bad at things. It is the starting point of something fantastic.

Did you learn to swim overnight?

Did you learn to ride a bike overnight?

Did you learn any skill overnight?

And that is the harsh reality. Although we want overnight success, we need time to develop a skill.

Take a deep breath and choose any skill. It might take time to become proficient, but each effort, each failure, is a step closer to mastery. And as you immerse yourself in this new venture, remember to strike a balance with life's other important aspects. Like I tell myself every time I open my laptop during a holiday, "It's a journey, and it's okay to take a break." So, take that first, imperfect step, and trust the process.

Starting with a new skill is daunting, but remember, Rome wasn't built in a day. The first step is to break down this new skill into smaller, more manageable tasks. This allows you to tackle it piece by piece, rather than getting overwhelmed by the whole picture.

A journey to financial freedom

Set achievable short-term goals that push you just beyond your comfort zone. This is where deliberate practice comes in. Instead of mindlessly repeating tasks, focus on your weaknesses. Make each practice session a conscious effort to improve.

And don't do it alone; feedback is invaluable. Whether it's from a mentor or through measurable outcomes, external feedback provides objective insight into your progress.

Consistency trumps intensity. A daily 30-minute practice session is often more effective than a once-a-week three-hour marathon. But also, be patient and kind to yourself. Progress will come, and setbacks are just stepping stones, not stumbling blocks.

***

"Lunch is ready. Hope you are hungry," Maja said. I switched focus from my computer. Oh, time passes. But I was grateful for the peaceful time I had to write. I looked around and saw Metodija was having his midday nap.

"Coming," I replied as I closed the laptop. I promised that I would not let this book completely consume my holiday.

I hope I can squeeze in a few more hours tonight and tell you how to start shaping and fine-tuning your skills.

Develop a skill

Key takeaways

- Be flexible in choosing a skill you want to grow – as it might change over time. It is not only normal but often advantageous.
- Choose a skill you like – even if you are not good at it. If you are going to spend 12–18 hours per day developing it, at least enjoy it.
- Don't overthink it – think about Analysis Paralysis. Tools like Pareto, time-boxing, and the two-route approach can help you in choosing the right skill.
- Even if your first choice doesn't pan out as you'd hoped, you're still moving forward, gaining experiences and insights that you wouldn't have had otherwise. You can afford to be wrong and try another skill.
- Although we want overnight success, we need time to develop a skill. Same as swimming.

Remember, your journey to financial freedom starts with a single step. It starts the moment you decide to embrace being "bad" as the starting point of becoming "good".

2. Start Freelancing

Monday. Day 3 in Malta. I am excited about the book and can't wait to dig deeper. We had a very long afternoon walk on Malta's coastline. The weather in October is perfect, neither hot nor cold. It's just perfect.

And once we returned, I was back in front of the laptop. I needed to get this book out of my system.

I talked with my friends, Zlatko and Vesna. They took a few days off from work to maximise our time together. I immediately got the feeling that I would have less time to

A journey to financial freedom

focus on the book, but I love spending time with friends and family.

It got me thinking. Do freelancers think about days off when they consider quitting their job and becoming full-time freelancers?

You see, as an employee, you have annual leave. It varies by country, but it is days you can take off and still get paid. As a freelancer, you just have days where you decide not to work, and you don't get paid for those days. Very different.

But I will get to those details later. Let's get back to the topic.

***

Now that you have chosen your skill, what is the next step towards financial freedom? Well, it's in the title of the chapter – you should become a freelancer.

Being a freelancer will help you be better at the skill you've chosen. It will give you the opportunity to work on multiple projects, broadening your experience. It will also enrich your portfolio, attracting even more clients.

My third trip to Malta wouldn't have been possible if I hadn't been a freelancer at the time. As a freelancer, I enjoyed the freedom to work from anywhere and set my own hours.

Start freelancing

I started my freelance journey with UpWork back in July 2011. UpWork is a platform connecting freelancers with companies that are looking for freelancers. Companies post details of projects or job ads, and freelancers bid for the project/job. As a freelance platform, it is a great starting opportunity for your freelance journey.

I was looking at multiple freelance platforms, and this one was really the best. It was a stepping stone for me, as I got access to so many business opportunities. I loved the fact that from Macedonia, I was able to work online and look for global freelance projects.

I was 24 and naïve when I started. I thought I could be a millionaire by 30. Let's laugh at that now. When I failed that, I was still ambitious and set my next target to be a millionaire by 35. Funny still.

Now I think I can be a millionaire by 40. Hopefully, this time I am right. If not, I can always push it to 45.

The first two services I offered on UpWork were market research and business planning. My experience? I had some, but I was far from an expert who could help other companies.

Interestingly, I didn't see it that way. I thought that I started a company at 21, and then at 24, I had three years of business experience and that made me an expert. So that was enough for me.

A journey to financial freedom

Looking back, I realise that my initial confidence was partly a result of what psychologists call the *Dunning-Kruger effect.*[2] For those unfamiliar with the term, it describes a cognitive bias where individuals with low ability at a task overestimate their ability. It's not that I was completely unaware or incompetent; rather, I didn't know what I didn't know. I mistook my limited experience for expertise, and that led me to take risks that I might not have taken otherwise. But here's the kicker: sometimes that irrational confidence is exactly what you need to take the first step.

While the Dunning-Kruger effect often has a negative connotation, in my case it served as a catalyst. It pushed me to put myself out there, to offer my services, and to start learning in a real-world context. The key is to combine this initial burst of confidence with an ongoing willingness to learn, adapt, and start recognising the areas where you genuinely need to improve and seek the necessary knowledge and skills.

Luckily enough, it also worked for clients.

I can vividly remember my first client. She came from a completely different time zone – Australia. It worked perfectly for me, as I was already a full-time employee, so I could meet the client late at night or early morning.

---

[2] Kruger, J.M. & Dunning, D. (1999). Unskilled and unaware of it: How difficulties in recognizing one's own incompetence lead to inflated self-assessments. Journal of Personality and Social Psychology, 77(12), 1121-1134.

Start freelancing

The job was a business plan for an immigration agency from Australia. And she had a budget of AU$100.

That first client taught me more than I could have ever learned from a textbook. Here's what happened: a few weeks after delivering the business plan, she reached back out to me. She had successfully secured a loan with the business plan I had written, and her immigration agency was officially in operation.

It was a light-bulb moment. Not only had I helped someone halfway around the globe, but I had also transformed a seemingly minor freelance gig into a life-changing opportunity for us both. That initial project became the cornerstone of my freelance portfolio, and it led to many more opportunities.

I still have no idea why she chose me, as I was not skilled enough to help her. Maybe I got lucky. And luck is an interesting perspective. For me, I believe I was lucky. But the client must have had some criteria in mind when she was interviewing multiple freelancers, and somehow, I fit best based on these criteria. Or maybe she chose me because of the low price. It is a perfect strategy for anyone starting in the freelance world.

That was my first freelance business plan, and I was so excited that I had started an additional income stream.

My freelance journey started with modest rates to attract clients and get a foothold in the marketplace. But, as I was not an expert in the field, I had to start from somewhere.

A journey to financial freedom

I got the opportunity to work on multiple projects. I sharpened my skills and got fantastic feedback.

As my freelance journey continued, I began to revisit the subject of pricing with increasing seriousness. I was under the common misconception that lower prices would keep me competitive; however, I soon realised this wasn't a sustainable or fair approach – especially as my skills and experience continued to grow.

Over time, I began to re-evaluate my value in the freelance market. I read books on pricing strategies, attended webinars, and even reached out to mentors in the industry for advice. With each completed project and satisfied client, my confidence grew, and I found myself inching closer to what I considered a fair rate for my services. It was a balancing act: price myself too low, and I'd undermine my worth but aim too high, and I'd risk scaring off potential clients.

As my portfolio expanded, I saw another shift: clients started coming to me. They had seen my work, read my reviews, and were willing to pay a fair price for my skills. It was no longer about being the cheapest option; it was about providing value. Slowly but surely, I increased my rates to reflect the quality of the work I was delivering. Clients were more than willing to pay for it.

The lesson here is not to undervalue yourself. Your skills are an asset, and as you grow in your freelance career, your pricing should reflect that. It's an evolving process, one

Start freelancing

that demands regular introspection and adjustment. But when you finally hit that sweet spot of value and worth, it will be an incredibly empowering milestone in your journey.

And it started from there. I felt the blood. In this case, it was extra money after work.

So there it is. The genesis of my freelance journey – a journey that began with limited expertise but an abundance of naïvety and enthusiasm. Whether it was setting laughably ambitious financial goals, underestimating my worth in pricing, or overestimating my expertise, each step, misstep, and adjustment was an invaluable lesson. Your journey will undoubtedly be different, filled with its own unique challenges and opportunities. But the principles remain the same: start somewhere, refine your skills, adjust your pricing, and most importantly, keep learning.

YOU DON'T NEED TO QUIT YOUR JOB

I will never encourage you to quit your job and become a freelancer. That would be the worst advice anyone could give to you.

The goal is to start freelancing part-time and, hopefully, in time, you'll grow to do this full-time. But until you get there, you have to pay the bills, too.

A journey to financial freedom

We have a saying here in Macedonia, "Don't spit in the old well until you finish digging the new one." So, it would help if you kept your job (and salary) until your side gig starts earning the same as your regular day job or even more.

I remember a friend who quit his job to dive full-time into freelance web development. Within a month, he found himself struggling to pay bills. His confidence dwindled, affecting the quality of his proposals and interactions with potential clients. It took him another six months of part-time jobs to stabilise himself financially and emotionally. So trust me, keep the old well running till the new one is ready.

Having a regular paycheck has its advantages. A full-time job offers a stable income that's predictable (if a bit boring).

After I finished college, I landed a stable job in a tech company. I felt secure but also trapped. I wanted to explore different sectors, different challenges. That's when I decided to freelance on the side. My monthly paycheck was my safety net, allowing me to be more selective with freelance gigs and build a portfolio at my own pace.

Freelance, on the other hand? Every new project you work on is a pure bonus, something you haven't planned. It's extra income to be used as a cash boost. Save for your apartment or plan a holiday – it's up to you.

Start freelancing

For me, freelance work was not just a one-time additional income; it added up to thousands over time, all supplementing my regular salary.

I remember my first major freelance payout. I'd just finished a long project and got paid €5,000, far more than my monthly salary at the time. I was ecstatic. I used the money to take a trip I'd always dreamed of, something I wouldn't have been able to afford otherwise.

Freelancing can be a bit more difficult at the beginning, especially if you are coming to it as an established expert. You have already established a price and are trying to get the same hourly rate on freelance platforms.

But on the freelance platforms, people don't know you. So, for them, you are a new guy without any experience.

So, consider this. Why would a client hire you – a 20-plus-year expert with zero feedback on the platform, against a three-year expert with 5-star feedback and a €100,000 portfolio already on the platform?

They have a problem, a task requiring someone to take care of it. And who should they give it to? It is a challenge for every client.

So, how do you compete with freelancers who have already built a reputation there? It's a catch-22.

One of my friends, Marija, is a seasoned designer. She decided to dip her toes into freelancing but found it incredibly tough at first. Despite her years of experience, she had

A journey to financial freedom

zero reviews on the freelance platform. She had to undercut her rates just to get her first few gigs. But she viewed it as a temporary sacrifice, an entry fee into the freelance world.

Consider it like this. If you work for one client, you get one experience in a year. But in the same year, if you work with 30–40 clients, you are becoming better at what you do.

You will have the opportunity to experience and work with different business models and see how you fit into each. It gives you an exponential experience as you learn and grow with each client. And it is how you become an expert in your field.

Depending on the field of expertise, the freelance world can be quite competitive. Use online resources, courses, or workshops to keep improving your skill set. Never get complacent; what's in demand today may not be tomorrow.

And to give you the bad news. In the beginning, you might find yourself working all the time. Being a full-time employee for eight hours, followed by an additional three to five hours, or more, working on your freelance career. It can be overwhelming. But don't get discouraged.

Mastering time management is your first key task. There are a lot of online tools available to help you plan your day to the minute. Allocate specific blocks of time to your

Start freelancing

day job, freelancing tasks, family, and even relaxation. Stick to this schedule religiously.

Create a dedicated workspace for freelancing. It doesn't have to be a separate room – just a quiet corner with a desk will do. When you sit there, you're at work. This helps mentally separate your day job from your freelance work and boosts productivity.

It is much easier to stay in the day job and complain. Complain about how the company should give you a better salary, how the government should give you some social benefits, how anyone should provide you with something. Well, guess what? Nobody gives away anything. You have to earn it.

Becoming better at specific skills can guarantee a higher salary – if that is what you are after.

FREELANCE SALES FUNNEL

A freelance gig requires consistency if you want to become a full-time freelancer. As such, you can view freelance work as a set of four activities.

First, you need to put a lot of effort into **finding and qualifying** the best freelance jobs. The more time you spend on qualifications – assessing whether the job is a good fit for you – the more relevant they will be. You don't want to spend a lot of additional energy to realise that you are not a good fit with the client.

A journey to financial freedom

Freelance platforms now have many advanced filters which could help you here. For example, you can shortlist the skills, categories, and price ranges to look only at qualified and relevant job ads. You can also look at the client's feedback from previous freelancers. That will save you a lot of time.

Second, you must **create engaging application forms** that differentiate you from fellow freelancers. Stop sending templates.

Each freelance job ad on freelance platforms gets 30–40 applicants. And you are one of them. So why you? What makes you unique?

Don't get me wrong. The client does not have an interest in knowing more about you. The client needs information about you to determine if you are the best person for the task. That's all. And you can use that, to focus the application on how you can help them.

Third, a **sales call or proposal** is the final part where you must shine – showing the client that you are the person for the job. Some clients would like to meet you on a call, while others will simply request a proposal. And if the price matches your skill set, you have a new client.

Fourth, you need to **overdeliver**. If you are in freelancing for the long game, you need to build relationships, not transactions. By overdelivering, you are showing the client that you genuinely want to help them, not just to charge them. And that opens the door for long-term collaboration, rather than a single project.

When you overdeliver, clients are happy. They give you additional work or recommend you to their friends or colleagues. So, overdelivering is a marketing tactic, bringing you many new projects.

And that is it. Optimise and repeat.

A journey to financial freedom

YOUR FREELANCE KPIS

Now that we've covered the four steps of successful free-lancing, let's look at what you need to become a full-time freelancer and the key metrics you should focus on. These key performance indicators (KPIs) will help you quantitatively measure your freelancing success and can give you insights on what areas need improvement. Key performance indicators will help you determine whether your freelance business is trending in the right direction.

The data that you need to collect from your freelance sales funnel is: a) Number of freelance applications submitted, b) Number of meetings booked or proposals sent, c) Number of new clients acquired, and d) The time the client stays with you. Based on this data, you can create 3 KPIs.

KPI #1: Meeting rate

How to measure: This KPI can be calculated by comparing the number of sales meetings/proposals against the number of freelance applications x 100.

Formula:

$$\text{Meeting Rate} = \frac{\text{Meetings Booked}}{\text{No. of Applications Sent}} \times 100$$

Why it matters: A higher meeting rate signifies that your freelance applications are effective and that prospects are

Start freelancing

interested in talking with you in more detail. And it is a starting point of the sales process, so the more sales calls with less applications the better. A 33% meeting rate means that out of ten freelance applications, you get three prospects to meet you.

How to improve:

- A low meeting rate could mean that your profile needs improvement. Clients look up your profile before deciding if they want to hear more from you.
- A/B test different application styles to see what resonates most with your potential clients. Some prefer long-form applications, while others prefer short and to the point.
- Spend more time customising each freelance application to suit the specific needs of the job.

KPI #2 Client acquisition rate

How to measure: This rate can be calculated by dividing the number of new clients acquired over a specific period, say a month, by the number of proposals sent or sales calls made during that time. Multiply by 100 to get a percentage.

Formula:

$$\text{Rate of Acquiring New Clients} = \frac{\text{No. of New Clients}}{\text{No. of Proposals Sent}} \times 100$$

A journey to financial freedom

Why it matters: A higher rate signifies that your sales calls or proposals are effective and that you're targeting the right type of clients. A low rate may indicate that your pitch needs refining or that you're not targeting the right opportunities. A 20% new client rate means that out of ten sales calls or proposals, you get two new clients.

How to improve:

- Spend more time customising each proposal to suit the specific needs of the job.
- Create social proof – building testimonials and case studies of previous clients could help you get more work.
- Consider playing with the price, as it might be the main reason why people are not deciding to work with you.

KPI #3 Client retention rate

How to measure: This is the percentage of clients who continue to work with you over a set period compared to the total number of clients you've worked with within the same time.

Formula:

$$\text{Client Retention Rate} = \frac{\text{No. of Clients Retained}}{\text{Total No. of Clients}} \times 100$$

Why it matters: A high retention rate means you're doing a great job meeting or exceeding client's expectations. A

Start freelancing

low rate is a red flag, indicating that you might need to reassess the quality of your work or your client management strategies.

How to improve:

- Conduct post-project reviews with your clients to get feedback.
- Consider offering loyalty discounts or referral incentives to encourage longer-term relationships.
- Add more services to your portfolio to keep the clients longer.

To give you an example, my cousin is a freelance writer who didn't pay much attention to client retention initially. She was great at landing new clients but didn't put in the extra effort to maintain those relationships. Eventually, she calculated her Client Retention Rate and was shocked to see it was only 20%. She reached out to past clients for feedback and made some changes based on their suggestions. Within three months, her Client Retention Rate shot up to 60%. She realised that sometimes it's not about finding new clients but nurturing the existing ones.

The goal of these KPIs is to ensure that you have a stable, ongoing flow in your freelance sales funnel. Please don't make the mistake I did. It is a stupid one. Early in my freelance career, I usually started by securing a few new clients, which would take eight to ten hours of my time daily. Then I focused on working on those projects. By the time the projects finished, I would realise that my sales

A journey to financial freedom

funnel was empty, as I was focused on serving my existing clients. Then, I would panic and start looking for work again. And unfortunately, there is a delay between deciding to look for a job and finding a new one.

One of my earliest freelance friends specialised in graphic design. She was so excited about landing her first big contract that she completely stopped looking for new projects. She did a fantastic job, but once the project wrapped up, she had nothing in the pipeline. It took her almost a month to find another client, which was a financially stressful period for her.

Here are some actionable tips to keep your funnel bustling with opportunities:

- Set a recurring reminder every week to spend at least two hours prospecting for new clients.
- Use a customer relationship management (CRM) system to track all client communications, so you don't let any opportunities slip through the cracks.
- Learn to say no: if your plate is full, it's better to turn down new work than to dilute the quality of your existing commitments.

Mastering your freelance sales funnel is not just about getting that initial gig; it's about creating a sustainable flow of opportunities that lets you take freelancing from a side hustle to a full-time career. It takes practice, diligence, and a bit of juggling, but you've got this.

Start freelancing

A FULL-TIME FREELANCER

Many people will stop here. A full-time job, supplemented with freelance projects, can give you a nice living. You will be focused on trading your time for money. If that is your goal – you've done it.

For me, the goal was to become a full-time freelancer. And it finally happened after four years of freelancing in 2015, at the worst possible time. As you grow older, your commitments get bigger, and it is harder and harder to switch from a stable salary into a risky freelance existence. It is much more challenging.

In 2015, at 28 years old, I already had a fiancée and bought a one-bedroom apartment. And it came with a huge mortgage. I am an economist, so I set the mortgage for five years. There was no way I was going to pay hefty interest rates accumulated over 30 years. In addition, our wedding was a few months ahead, and we were looking for honeymoon destinations.

Looking back, I am glad that I took that step then. At the time of writing, I am 36, I have a much bigger mortgage, a five-year-old, and a second child on the way. So, it gets harder over the years. And I can only assume how much harder it would get at 40 or 50 to make that transition.

A friend of mine waited until his early 50s to consider freelancing full-time. By then, his commitments were far too overwhelming: a mortgage, two kids in college, and a

59

A journey to financial freedom

stable yet unfulfilling job. He found the prospect of leaving that stability for the Wild West of freelancing too daunting. His transition became a now-or-never situation, and he chose never. His story serves as a reminder that the best time to transition is when you can afford to take calculated risks.

If you're ready to make the leap, get the following in place:

1. **Client retention plan:** Before quitting your day job, make sure you have a plan for retaining your existing clients. Loyal clients can provide stability in the initial uncertain months.

2. **Cash reserve:** Make sure you have at least three months' worth of living expenses saved. Freelancing income can be unpredictable, especially at the beginning.

3. **Skills inventory:** Take a thorough inventory of your skills and identify areas where you could offer additional services or improve. A broader skill set can make you more marketable.

4. **Set boundaries:** Decide in advance what your working hours will be and how you'll separate work time from personal time to avoid burnout.

5. **Insurance and benefits:** Research and plan how you'll cover essentials like health insurance, which you may lose after quitting a full-time job.

6. **Business structure:** Decide on your freelance business structure – sole proprietorship, LLC, etc. – and consider a tax advisor to help you set up.

7. **Financial tracking system**: Set up a system for tracking income, expenses, and invoices. Consider software or consult a bookkeeper.

COST-BENEFIT ANALYSIS

Why did I become a full-time freelancer? Well, quite simply. The math didn't add up. As an economist, I learned that a cost-benefit analysis is always a good decision-making tool. And now, I want to use it in the context of full-time freelancing *vs.* full-time employment.

I was working in a software company, so the salary was excellent (within the top 1% in Macedonia).

But I was also getting better and better at freelancing. Over four years, I have done many projects and sharpened my skills. I was becoming better not just at execution skills but also at applying for projects, negotiating terms, and selling. Finally, I became good at the freelance game, which eventually was followed by increasing my price.

I looked at **job satisfaction**. At one point, I worked for eight hours in an office, trying to negotiate between developers and the sales team. It was exhausting, as both sides believed their view was more important. And don't get me started about bugs, pissed-off clients, revisions, and product documentation.

A journey to financial freedom

And then, after work, I would spend four hours or more doing what I love – working with entrepreneurs and helping them shape their businesses. At one moment, I am talking to a Californian startup that wants to create a mobile app for face/mood recognition. I am working with a Middle East startup that wants to offer procurement as a service to the oil industry. Each project was more exciting than the previous one.

I remember working on a project that involved designing a gamification strategy for a health app to motivate users to live a healthier lifestyle. Then, the very next project was for a financial startup looking to simplify investment choices. The diversity kept me engaged and excited every single day.

So when it came to job satisfaction, freelancing won.

Then I looked at the **financial aspect**. I was earning more money after work than my full-time job. So, it meant that I would make much more money if I had full-time work with freelance projects. But that is a big if, as it comes with a lot of insecurity compared to a stable paycheck. And believe me, the older you get, the harder the decision is to move away from your comfort zone into freelancing.

But what won me over toward full-time freelancing was the **flexibility**. As a freelancer, you choose your pace.

Of course, you can work from anywhere. I quit my job right before my wedding, so I went on a 45-day honeymoon trip with my wife: a road trip around Europe. It was

Start freelancing

amazing to see Austria, Germany, Netherlands, France, Italy, Croatia, and the entire coastline of the Adriatic Sea. I would visit a new city, do some sightseeing in the morning, and then do some work in the afternoon. I didn't come back rich, but I could cover my travel expenses and have decent food on the table.

And after two months, I went for another 30 days' vacation on the Black Sea. I learned that in September, resorts are much more affordable. So, we stayed for 30 days on the beach. We were at the beach until lunchtime and worked in the afternoon and night.

I don't think I would ever be able to go back to 20 days' annual holiday. It is simply not enough.

When I was making the cost-benefit analysis, what helped me tremendously was the **strategic aspect** of the decision. On the one hand, when you start working full-time as a freelancer, you are building an asset. If clients are happy with you, they recommend you and give you more work. With time, in a few years as a full-time freelancer, you will have a great portfolio. At that stage, clients will start coming to you. In addition, over time, you are building assets that will stay forever.

On the other hand, if I stayed at my job, I could only progress in my career, building the company's assets. I earn a salary for what I do, but eventually, in three, five or even ten years, I can lose my job. And except for the earned

A journey to financial freedom

money, I won't have anything to keep and need to search for a new job.

But don't get me wrong, it's not all rainbows and butterflies in the freelancing world. And I must give you a fair warning about the bad parts of this journey, too, so you'll be prepared.

Uncertainty is something that you must be comfortable with. For example, you have too much work today but might have none in a week. Or you might have a dry month and then have three months' work that you need to finish in one month.

It can be pretty stressful if you can't cope with uncertainty. However, it does help if you put some savings aside for "dry" days. You'll thank me later. It doesn't need to be a lot, but having a few months' worth of living expenses can help. This fund can act as a financial cushion for slower months and offer peace of mind.

And another mistake is people are moving to freelance because they don't want to have a **manager to tell them what to do**.

Well, guess what. When you are a full-time employee, you have only one manager. And as a full-time freelancer, you can handle three to five projects in parallel. And that means managing three to five different managers at the same time. So, if you are bad at listening to directions and feedback, you will have problems.

64

Start freelancing

And finally, the worst part, at least for me, is that you no longer have guaranteed **annual leave**. It took me some time to adjust my mindset to this. In Macedonia, when you work for a company, you have annual leave that is guaranteed by law.

As a freelancer, you could have infinite holidays. It's just unpaid. And that hurts. So, if you go on holiday for a week, it is not just the expenses for those seven days that you need to plan for. It is also the missed income for the work you could have done if you hadn't taken that holiday.

It took me four years in my freelance journey to finally be comfortable about quitting my job and continuing as a full-time freelancer.

Of course, if I had known I was on that journey, I would have focused more on freelancing and done it in far less time. But nobody told me. And this is why I am writing

A journey to financial freedom

this book to help you and anyone like you considering leaving the full-time job and starting a journey in the free-lance world.

And being a full-time freelancer could be the end of the road for some of you. Being well paid, flexible working hours. Is it enough?

Well, only you know the answer to this.

But if you are ambitious and don't want to stop here, you have to figure out a way to earn money, not based on the hours you put in. But to make money based on the assets you own, and the time others put in. It is the only way to reach financial freedom.

***

"Are you coming for dinner? Zlatko is making your favourite food," Maja asked. I had a few more things to share, but perhaps it is just enough to show you the way.

"Five more minutes, and I am coming," I said. I rushed ahead to the next chapter and made several bullet points that I wanted to address. The biggest struggle as an author is getting started. When you wake up and see a blank page, it is hard to begin. So, the trick is to create bullet points for the next chapter whenever you finish a chapter. This way, you don't stare at a blank chapter the next day; you have a starting point.

I have tried it, and it works.

Start freelancing

KEY TAKEAWAYS

- The best way to shape the skill you've chosen is to start freelancing. Freelance platforms (like UpWork) are the best starting point to find international projects.
- The freelance world can be quite competitive. You can start with modest rates to attract clients, sharpen your skills, and get fantastic feedback.
- Don't quit your job. Start as a part-time freelancer. Refine your skills, adjust your pricing, and most importantly, keep learning. As you become better, clients will start reaching out to you.
- Don't spit in the old well until you finish digging the new one. Having a monthly paycheck can be your safety net, allowing you to be more selective with freelance gigs.
- Consider freelancing as a sales funnel that requires consistency in a) Finding and qualifying freelance jobs, b) creating engaging application forms, c) making sales calls or proposals, and d) overdelivering.
- When you overdeliver, clients are happy. They give you additional work or recommend you to their friends or colleagues. So, overdelivering is a marketing tactic, bringing you many new projects.

A journey to financial freedom

- Having freelance KPIs will help you measure your freelancing success and give you insights into what areas need improvement.

- Want to be a full-time freelancer? Create your own cost-benefit analysis. Aspects like job satisfaction, financials, job flexibility, strategy are just a few. Also, consider uncertainty, multi-management and annual leave before deciding if it is the right step for you.

Remember, becoming a full-time freelancer is like running a mini-business – solopreneur. But even if you are still paid for the hours you work, it is a step toward your financial freedom.

3. Become An Entrepreneur

Tuesday. Somehow Tuesday got filled with family activities. I believe that is one of the main reasons why people choose the entrepreneurial route – the ability to choose your own priorities.

After breakfast, we spent the whole day at the beach. Golden Bay is among the best beaches in Malta, with crystal clear water.

And we had a lot of fun. Metodija couldn't stop playing with the sand, the waves, and all the beach toys we brought. He even met a girl. Kids at that age are so funny, especially when they like each other.

In the evening we ordered some Balkan BBQ for dinner. I prepared the salad, and we had a couple of shots of rakia. Rakia is the collective term for fruit spirits (or fruit brandy) popular in the Balkans. Balkan folks sip rakia whenever they get the chance, mainly at celebrations. And sometimes the occasion is that it is Monday or Tuesday.

However, needless to say, I didn't get another chapter written. I felt guilty. Although I appreciate my freedom, and I am able to travel and do sightseeing, I made a commitment to write this book. But family comes first.

On **Wednesday** I woke up at 5:00am, determined to create the Entrepreneur chapter. I poured myself a cup of hot coffee, and while everyone else was sleeping, it was time to reflect on my transition from a full-time freelancer to an entrepreneur. For the first time, I experienced what it means to increase my income by using other people's time – a critical step toward financial freedom.

BEYOND FREELANCING

Being a full-time freelancer is nice. The flexibility, the premium rates, and everything else. But the journey should not stop here for you.

Become an entrepreneur

And for me, it was a normal evolution. As you become better and more comfortable with your skills, clients will start noticing that and will keep giving you more work.

And if you keep your sales funnel consistent, you'll always have work. But often, you will have more work than you can handle.

In the beginning, for me, this was normal. Whenever there is more work, I would work more than eight hours, and that is it. Sometimes 10, sometimes 12, and in rare cases, 20 hours in a single day.

And at that time I was still happy, as every extra hour directly impacted on my income. If you do it occasionally, it's great.

But at some point, I had more work than I could handle for more than three months.

I prided myself on delivering high-quality work, always. But there was this one week where I had overbooked myself, thinking I could handle it all.

I was working around the clock, grabbing short naps here and there. Finally, I sent off a business plan project to a long-term client. He wasn't happy; the quality wasn't up to the usual standard. His feedback was a wake-up call.

I had risked a long-term relationship for short-term gains. The stress and the lack of sleep had caught up with me, impacting the very thing that mattered most – my work. That experience was a loud and clear signal that I needed

A journey to financial freedom

help. I couldn't continue to stretch myself thin and expect to maintain high standards.

That is when I realised I needed external help – someone who could help me and take some of the workload from me.

In addition, being overbooked started affecting my ability to take holidays, which was one of the main motivations for moving to freelancing. And that started fading out as more and more work came in.

Eventually, as I continued with my freelance sales funnel, I started rejecting job offers. And that hurt. You put a lot of effort into your freelance funnel in case you run out of work. And then, there's a potential client, waving cash in hand, and it is tempting to take that job as well. Maybe you can squeeze them in, put in a few extra hours, and further increase your income.

I remember a time when I received a call from a client who was extremely excited about a new project. It was a high-profile job, the kind of work that could serve as a flagship case study for years to come. My heart sank when I looked at my already-packed calendar.

With much regret, I had to turn it down. As I hung up the phone, the weight of that decision fully sank in. It wasn't just a missed opportunity for income; it was a missed opportunity for growth, recognition, and expanding my portfolio. That was the moment I knew I couldn't continue as a lone freelancer if I wanted to seize opportunities that were coming my way.

But this is a never-ending story. There is always a new client around the corner with an exciting project, flashing his credit card.

And it hurts thanking them but rejecting the project. It further increases the desire to hire external help if only you had someone to alleviate some of the workload.

MY ENTREPRENEURIAL VISION

But then it dawned on me. What if I start a business? What if I hire full-time employees? The thought is quite seductive: registering a company, hiring a few people full-time, and becoming the leader. There's an undeniable ego boost in managing a team and steering the ship.

I immediately pictured myself being a business owner, working hand-in-hand with employees, being able to achieve so much more.

However, the transition from a freelancer to being an employer comes with its set of challenges. It's not just about your work anymore. There are so many other things that you need to take care of: accounting, HR, operations, marketing, and sales. These are skill sets you'll need to either acquire or outsource, adding layers of complexity to your work-life balance.

A journey to financial freedom

Moreover, the financial risk of owning a company extends beyond your own livelihood. Employees need their salaries regardless of the business's financial standing. You're not just bringing food to your table but also to your employees', not to mention meeting your tax obligations.

My vivid vision of owning a company was now seen through a haze of fear and uncertainty. There are so many things that could go wrong.

But then, there are other routes for obtaining help without jumping full into starting a business. What if you hired a freelancer or brought in part-time help? It felt like it was an in-between stage where I could still get help without starting a business.

When I decided to hire a freelancer, I thought it was going to be smooth sailing. Just pass them the work and get it done, right? But I quickly learned that even freelancers require a certain level of management and quality control. I had one project go sideways because I didn't adequately vet a freelancer's skills. Thankfully, it was a small project, but it taught me a valuable lesson on the importance of quality control when outsourcing.

Managing freelancers can be both simple and complicated. The idea is straightforward: find a reliable freelancer, delegate tasks, and focus on your specialised skills. Depending on your level of confidence in their abilities, you can assign them either a portion of the project or the

Become an entrepreneur

entire project. In both ways, your role shifts from doing everything in the project to quality control and oversight.

My initial thought was that I could get a cheaper freelancer to do the job for me, and I would deliver it to the client and make a profit margin. In hindsight, I realise how naïve I was to think that it would be that simple.

Hiring external help doesn't mean adding services that you cannot do or adding complementary services to your own. It is nothing like that.

It is about finding help that can do exactly or partially what you do so that you can step away from operations. One option is to give parts (30–70%) of the project to a third party, which is most commonly the essential part. Then you, as an expert, can take those 30–70% and finish them to 100%. This way, you are confident that the project is done as you would have done; just someone helped you.

Alternatively, you can find a freelancer to do 100% of the job. Then, you only need to review and ensure they didn't miss anything, as you need to sign off before delivering to the client.

In both cases, the client can, but it doesn't have to know that you have other people involved in doing the project. And from experience, as long as you deliver top quality and are honest, in most cases, they don't care who was working on the project. So, it is up to you to review, ensure quality check, and commit that the client always gets the best results possible.

A TASTE OF BEING A LEADER

I wanted to play it safe – ensure minimum risks in my outsourcing journey. So, the first external support was my wife, Maja. I thought, if it has to be someone, it should be someone I trust. And it helped to keep the whole income in the family.

Maja has a background in business logistics, so she quickly understood some bits of the work I was doing for the clients. In four or five years of listening to me talking about it over dinner, she was already up to speed with my freelance work.

In addition, as we live under the same roof, it was pretty easy to work together, and if she had questions or got stuck, I could quickly jump in and help. So, I was excited when she agreed to work with me.

But is it a good idea to work with your wife? I had quite some doubts at the beginning, to be honest.

If you share the same doubts, let me give you some of the challenges but also some advantages.

Become an entrepreneur

First, it might **consume your private lives**. I mean, spending eight hours at work with your wife and then coming back home, there is not much else to discuss.

"How was your day?" I asked this question several times, more as a joke, as we spent most of the day together.

And guess what we are talking about during dinner, travelling, or even on holiday? Work, work, and work. Yes, we also talked about other stuff, but somehow, work was pretty much the main topic.

I thought it could be a serious problem, but it wasn't. It somehow aligned, and although we work together, we always had time to forget about work, discuss personal stuff, and raise a family.

Secondly, it is pretty **hard to be a manager and a husband**. People make mistakes at work. And as a manager, I can be agitated with an employee, but if I try to do this to my wife, I might sleep in the garage. This is a great inside joke I have with my wife.

It is also hard when I need to take off the management hat and become a husband after work. As many of us, we carry our work role into our private lives, too.

But we had a strong partnership and we aligned ourselves quickly to our new situation.

And finally, you are **on the same ship** – which can be advantageous and disadvantageous. It is excellent when we have enough work, but our whole family suffers if we

A journey to financial freedom

come to a minimal or zero work period as we both bring food from the same business.

That is a risk that, luckily, I never had to experience, but it is a thought I had in the back of my mind for quite some time. Something that kept me awake at night.

Enough about the fears. Let me share some of the **advantages**.

If I am a freelancer and my wife is a full-time employee, I can **travel** whenever I want. But she can't. So then I can't either, which defies the whole purpose of freedom and flexibility.

Since we were both freelancing, we had the freedom to work from anywhere. And we did. Besides our 45-day work and travel around Europe for our honeymoon, we spent a month in Bulgaria working together from a rented apartment. And as we were now working together, we could plan our workload so that we can take some time off together.

Ah yeah, and the **income doubled**. Having two people work as freelancers helped us a lot – financially. My wife didn't need to start from scratch, as I already had the portfolio, the reference, and the credibility, and she was just in the background directly working on the projects. And she was great at being a freelancer.

To sum it up, I don't have any regrets about deciding to include my wife in our joint freelancing/digital nomad

Become an entrepreneur

journey. We had our ups and downs, but we addressed them together.

Having my wife as a **first external person** helped a lot. I was able to afford to make management & organisational mistakes, use the learning curve, and optimise the process.

Pros & Cons
working with your spouse

✓ It's somebody you trust

✓ Helps double the family income

✓ Likely up to speed with the work already

✓ Managerial mistakes have lesser impact

✓ Travel freely, work anywhere

✗ You are on the same ship – for better or for worse ✓

Work might consume your private lives ✗

Pretty hard being a manager & husband ✗

In software terms, it was really like a beta version, as I was able to obtain the feedback that I needed. And I am very grateful that my wife agreed to this journey. I highly doubt I would be even halfway where I am now without her. You see, I am a front-end person, talking to clients, negotiating, selling, and pitching. I love the limelight. Maja, on the other hand, is the back-end person, organising contracts, invoices, and directly working on projects. A perfect balance.

A journey to financial freedom

***

I was distracted by the alarm that went off. Is it 8am already? Ah, I got myself deep into the book and lost track of time.

"I am going to the shop for groceries. Do you need anything?" I asked Maja as I was getting dressed.

"Eggs and cheese please, for breakfast," she replied.

I took the longer route to the shop, using the opportunity to have a coffee at a coffee shop directly looking over the coastline of Sliema.

It is so nice when you wake up at 5am and have the morning for yourself.

The rest of the week in Malta was reserved for holiday activities.

We spent some quality time in Valletta, the capital of Malta. We visited the famous St. John Cathedral. With its colossal grandeur and breathtaking beauty, this baroque gem never fails to leave me in awe.

We were taking sightseeing slowly as Maja was in her 7th month of pregnancy. But we are quite the adventurers, so nothing could stop us from enjoying our day in Valletta to the fullest.

I managed to go to Gozo, enjoy the Blue Hole, and go to Il Camino, the famous blue lagoon beach. We went to Cisk Factory in the afternoon, where Zlatko and Vesna

Become an entrepreneur

work. As you may be already guessing, the other chapters of the book I was planning to write were still blank. I didn't do any additional work.

And here I was on Saturday, packing to go back home. A week has passed. I initially hoped that I would be able to write the whole book. Instead, I barely wrote half.

This is still good, as that means that in one week, I managed to enjoy myself in Malta and still create half a book from scratch.

And here I am getting on the plane again.

"Boarding has completed," the flight attendant said as I took my seat.

Earlier today, I bought myself a Bluetooth keyboard for only one reason – to use the flight from Malta to Macedonia (almost two hours) to write. And I can't pick up the laptop, as the seats are small, but I can type on my phone with a Bluetooth keyboard. This is how committed I am when it comes to this book.

The plane was taking off, and I was ready to continue.

A journey to financial freedom

SCALING THE FREELANCE POOL

As I had a fantastic positive experience with my first external (or, in my case, internal) help, I started considering how to scale this process.

How can I have a pool of two, five, or ten freelancers? And I am using the word "pool" carefully, as I was not planning on paying them full-time. I wanted to know the people and their expertise, so I could hire them ad hoc to help me with the workload when a project came in.

Having a team of external freelancers. A dream come true. But is it?

This is when I really started understanding the value my clients see in me and my freelance work. It is quite tough to find a good freelancer. Like, really hard.

I found it funny. Now that I have to look for freelancers, I am the client. And all the complaints I made toward my clients as a freelancer, I should start receiving the same. So, it does require a shift in your mindset.

Think about clients you enjoyed working with, and start acting like one. Don't be the tough, sentimental, and childish client complaining about everything, just hoping to get a discount. Be the client that looks for long-term collaborators rather than short-term wins.

As I wrote earlier, you should look at your freelancers as potential long-term work partners, the same way as you would clients.

Do you know how much effort it takes to replace an existing freelancer with a new one? Building the trust and the level of quality you want?

So, as you are the client in a freelancer's eyes, don't be one of the lousy clients we all have worked for.

RECRUITING THE RIGHT TEAM

Now let me share the story of how I started recruiting on freelance platforms. I posted a job ad for the first time, looking for people to help me. As I was deep in the work, I knew pretty well what kind of people I needed and what types of skill sets they should possess. So, it was pretty straightforward to me.

After my first request for help, I received more than 50 applicants from around the world.

How am I supposed to know which are the good ones and which are the not-so-good ones?

Should I interview all 50 of them?

How much time should I dedicate to this recruitment process?

A journey to financial freedom

And then it hit me. It is precisely the same feeling that my potential clients face when selecting the right candidate, the right fit for the job.

That helped me a lot. I could use all the thoughts and insights I experienced as a potential client in my future job applications as a freelancer, as I knew how they felt. I knew they were struggling to choose among dozens of freelancers, trying to figure out the best fit for them.

So, I changed my freelance application process. Instead of telling potential clients about me, my experience and my expertise, I chose a different approach. I started talking about them, about their problems and in between, I pitched in a couple of nice words about myself, too.

I stopped writing about how much experience I had, my diplomas and all my flattering reviews. Instead, I started talking about them. About how they would solve their problems if they hired me. Here are some bits of the proposals I had sent:

"Are you in the consultancy world? Interestingly so, I work with a few consultants from the same industry. So, I understand your pains and how hard it is to run a consultancy business. As I worked with several consultants, these are the results I've managed to achieve for them."

"Are you from the UK? Excellent, I am currently doing several projects for other UK clients, and this is what we do and the results we are achieving."

Can you spot the difference? Although I was tailoring the messages to them, I was still explaining how I would help. The conversation was far smoother when presenting credibility, reference, and social proof – especially if it is from a similar/same industry or country.

When I started reviewing for potential freelancers, I had to figure out a methodology, as I couldn't interview 50-plus people. I should note that this methodology worked for me as I was looking for an inexperienced freelancer with a lower hourly rate. My goal was to hire people that I could teach and delegate some of my project activities to them.

So, my first disqualification criterion was taking out anyone beyond my budget. This was easy, as I knew my budget, and if I was to make any margin, I had to set boundaries. Of course, if I could afford more expensive experienced freelancers, I could have charged more, but that was not my goal at the time.

A journey to financial freedom

The second was to disqualify anyone with a generic message as if they didn't put any effort into tailoring the application message to me. Why should I put the effort into reviewing them? Another lesson learned that I applied to my freelance application process.

The third thing I did was to examine their proficiency in English. It is hard to communicate with a long-term supplier if there is a language barrier.

I narrowed it down to several candidates and booked the meetings.

As a freelancer, whenever someone booked a meeting with me, I prepared and researched the client. This way I could impress and show them that I made an extra effort. So, I was expecting the same from the people that I was interviewing.

And for the first time now, I didn't need to prepare. The candidates were the ones who were supposed to impress me, not the other way around.

I started interviewing and realised how hard it would be to find the right people. Some of the freelancers were completely lost in space.

They acted like someone else had applied for them, and they had no idea what the job was about. The application message they sent was perfect, but the actual interviews were awful.

Become an entrepreneur

I realised how smart a decision it was to interview the applicants personally. If I had made a decision based solely on their applications, I would be completely screwed. There were a few OK freelancers and even fewer great ones. It was a tough call, but I picked a few and hired them through UpWork.

There were some things that I did not consider when hiring freelancers.

First, I was now a manager in addition to working on projects and maintaining my freelance sales flow. And that takes time.

Sometimes, a client was unclear with their instructions, or the freelancer misunderstood the task, and we had to do the work from scratch. Sometimes, freelancers were busy on other projects, so I had to wait far longer than anticipated, delaying the overall project and making the client nervous.

I could somehow manage all that. But delivering a consistent level of quality was my biggest concern. I had several freelancers, and I had to review all the work they did to ensure that they were delivering the desired quality.

Most freelancers were working after their full-time job (something I had done in the past), and they were already exhausted. Their mistake rate was quite high, and that was taking me more time to fix. They were juggling multiple freelance projects, so I was not always on their priority list. Even if I requested some minor changes that could

A journey to financial freedom

take one hour, I still waited two or three days for an update. It was the price I had to pay for choosing inexperienced freelancers with a lower hourly rate.

Even with freelancers, I still had complete ownership of the projects. So, rather than delegating projects, I was delegating tasks, and as I was still the owner, I had to go over each completed task to ensure the quality. This way I was still responsible to the client for the outcome of the project.

One late night, as I was going over all the mistakes the freelance team has made and going over long business plans, I came to a realisation.

If I really wanted to grow the business, I needed full-time people in-house. People who would work full time on the projects and not after work hours.

I needed people to be available full-time for revisions, quality improvements, and modifications.

People who I would put extra effort into training at the beginning, and then I could utilise that knowledge in the long term.

At that point, it became obvious that I needed to start a business. There was no other way. It was the more expensive way, as I needed to get an office and equipment and pay bills and salaries. It was a decision that came with a

Become an entrepreneur

lot of risks. But you know what they say: "The riskier the road, the greater the profit."[3]

It was the harder way, as I couldn't afford experienced people, so the only way this could work was to find new, inexperienced people and teach them. So, like it or not, I had to evolve my entrepreneurial journey into becoming a start-up.

***

"Cabin crew, prepare for landing." I had to stop here. I needed to turn off my Bluetooth and stop my focused work on the book.

And maybe this was for the better. I needed to defocus from the book for a bit and leave space for new thoughts and ideas that will make this book even better. Now, I will take some time to reflect and enrich it with more examples. Quality over quantity – it has always been my motto.

"Cabin crew, we are ready for landing," was the last thing I listened to before I closed my keyboard.

I glanced at Maja and saw that both her and Metodija were sleeping. I was pleased that they are resting, and I had the time to focus on finishing this chapter.

---

[3] Behr, I. S. (1995). The Star Trek: Deep Space Nine: The Ferengi Rules of Acquisition. United States: Pocket Books/Star Trek.

A journey to financial freedom

Key takeaways

- As much as it hurts, sometimes you need to reject a job offer. Don't ever sacrifice project quality just for the sake of saying yes to more projects.
- Getting external part-time help is a great next step before deciding to start a business.
- At the beginning, start hiring cheap and inexperienced freelancers. As you grow, you can get more skilled ones.
- Think about clients you've enjoyed working with, and start acting like one. Be the client that looks for long-term collaborators rather than short-term wins.
- Consider working with your spouse – a financial freedom journey should be a mutual goal, and it comes with many advantages.
- Create recruitment criteria that work for you, and start hiring accordingly.

Remember, as an entrepreneur, you don't earn from the hours you work, but from the hours others put in. A critical change in how you generate your income, a step closer to financial freedom.

PART II:

STARTING A BUSINESS

4. Register A Startup

November 2022. Time seems to stand still when you're waiting in line, but when you're doing something you love or you're having a great time, it flies. It seemed like I had barely blinked, and it was already November. Two weeks had passed since my rejuvenating holiday in Malta, and the promise of my book project still loomed large in my thoughts.

The day we returned, my son Metodija experienced his first serious fall. For a parent, there's nothing scarier than

A journey to financial freedom

seeing your child in pain and covered in blood. He smashed his chin, and we had to rush to the ER. He needed stitches. I was shaking with fear. It reminded me of the fear of the unknown I felt when I decided to start my business.

Post-Malta life was quite busy. I had a few workshops lined up; I was a keynote speaker at AllWeb Albania. After my trip to Albania, I had to immediately repack for yet another trip – this time to Armenia for an entrepreneurship workshop with an eight-hour layover in Vienna.

So, there I was, in the business lounge at Vienna airport. It was my first time there, so I felt like Alice in Wonderland. I've learned something new today. Business lounges are impressive. It took me 36 years to realise this. I was travelling to Armenia with Monika and Dimitar – we were all US alumni, invited to the training in Armenia. Thanks to Monika and her platinum credit card, I was in the business lounge – all inclusive. I was able to get a lot of work done. Mind-blowing for me. Not sure how I haven't figured this out earlier.

However, let's return to the point of this chapter – the transition from being an entrepreneur to making the decision and start a company. Registering a start-up is the logical next step after you've proven yourself as an entrepreneur. It is the only way you can formalise your business and be able to scale even faster.

Register a startup

LOOK AT THE WORST-CASE SCENARIO

As I said, it can be quite scary. For me, this was a decision shadowed by a storm of stress and uncertainty. Doubts swirled around my head like a relentless whirlwind, clouding my thoughts and eclipsing my clarity. Each "what if?" was a drop of worry that swelled into a tempest of anxiety within my mind.

What if it doesn't work? What if I don't have enough work for all the employees? What if I hire the wrong people? So many questions were in my head.

But what was the alternative? How could I evolve and expand my freelance endeavour when the quality and commitment were hanging by a thin thread? How can I grow my freelance business if I can't control the quality and get full-time commitment from the team?

I had two options. I could keep delaying the decision forever and stay where I was in my cosy comfort zone, but drowning in work and failing to meet the deadlines and the quality of work I used to deliver to clients, or I could take a leap of faith and jump into the unknown, cold water.

I had to make up my mind and do it ASAP. Time waits for no one, and every second that passed I'm losing money. But don't get me wrong. I am not a gambler, randomly placing a bet on my business. I did my calculations,

95

A journey to financial freedom

my research and analysed my risks thoroughly. It wasn't a sudden nor an easy move.

Let me tell you exactly how I made that decision and found the courage to start BizzBee Solutions.

It was early 2016. I was driving with Maja from Skopje to Belgrade. It was before we had kids, so we were alone in the car for five hours. We often take road trips, especially when we need to make some decisions.

If I'm driving, I can't use the internet or do something with my hands. So, I talk. I mean, talk a lot. It's a smart way of focusing on one topic.

And the topic in our ten-hour return trip was whether we should start a business. We were already established freelancers, and we needed to decide if we wanted to take it to the next step. We spent five to six hours discussing the advantages and disadvantages.

Register a startup

The most obvious positive aspect was the finances. We thought we would get rich just like that. How naïve were we? Of course, having a formal business would enable us to work with more companies outside freelancing. And it would help us grow our current operations, meaning more employees, which would lead to more money. That was the plan, at least.

And formalising our business would also mean that we could take on employees. People that could deliver the work while I could take a step back and work less. Or have more holidays.

It also meant we would be able to provide better quality. I could invest time and energy into teaching our employees, ensuring that their quality of work is at a really high level.

But there were also disadvantages.

Hiring more people would mean more costs, for sure. And that would put pressure on me, as we have to ensure salaries, regardless of how much work we have.

Another scary aspect was that this company was our joint source of income. If the source was to dry up, we would both be left with no money.

As we married less than a year ago, a child was also in the conversation. How could we focus on raising a family if we were now starting a business? Could we do both? We

97

A journey to financial freedom

were still pretty young. Were we biting off more than we could chew? Were we crazy?

This conversation went on and on for hours. The bottom line was that we both lacked the courage to take that jump at this point.

But there and then, a light bulb went on above my head.

"Let's try one more approach before we give up," I said.

"Let's look at it from another angle. What is the worst that could happen if we start a business and fail within three months of starting?"

"What do you mean?" Maja was not sure.

"Well, what will happen if we decide to start the business? Get an office, hire a few people, equipment, and everything we need, and run the business for three months. For example, hire four people plus the two of us."

"Well, worst case scenario, we would have zero new clients and be a lot in debt. It can't be worse than that. We can try and fail," Maja answered, as it is the most logical answer.

"Yes, that would be the worst-case scenario. Can we now put this on the map? Can we quantify it, so I would know how bad it would be? I want to be able to assess each of the risks and costs."

Register a startup

And as I was driving, Maja took out a small notepad and started making calculations, still in the car, in a different country, and without internet access.

First, we will need an **office**. As offices are expensive, we can find a residential apartment and adjust it into an office. As 100% of our clients are from abroad, we don't need a luxury downtown office building. A two-bedroom apartment will be enough. In our neighbourhood, at that time it was €200/month. So, we needed €600 worth of rent for the next 3 months.

Next, we will need some **furniture and equipment** for that office. As our budget is tight, do we need brand-new furniture? Of course not. It is a three-month experiment. We estimated that with €500, we could get six decent second-hand desks and a few drawers. Next, we'll need chairs. We'll go to IKEA, and we can surely find some good ones for €50. So, €300 for six people.

Then, the **equipment**. A decent PC was around €400 per person. Luckily, I can continue working on my laptop, and Maja can keep the home computer to minimise costs. So, we need only four sets – €1,600 in total for equipment.

To summarise, furniture and equipment were estimated at €3,000. Seeing this number, I couldn't help but feel a mix of excitement and fear. This wasn't just money; it was our hard work, our dreams, and our future. It was a big risk, but we believed in what we were doing.

A journey to financial freedom

And then, we needed to hire the employees, of course. Hiring experienced people would be too big of a cost at this point. Well, what if we look for four interns instead of taking on experienced staff? Fresh from school but ambitious and eager to learn? At the time, most of the internship opportunities were free for three months. We've agreed to cover at least €50 for travel costs. That would be €200 for all four interns per month or €600 for three months.

Summarising, it was €600 for renting the office space, €2,400 for equipment and furniture, and €600 for salaries for three months. So, we got to a total number of €3,600.

Even if we add additional money for a printer, setting up the office, network, etc., any calculation that we threw into the notepad was below €5,000.

Don't get me wrong. Maybe my numbers would sound awfully low or pretty high, depending on where you are based. At that time, Macedonia had very low prices, which meant lower starting costs. But at that point in my life, it felt like a lot of money to risk in starting a business.

The numbers might be higher or lower, depending on where you are from, but the thought process is the same in understanding your worst-case scenario.

"OK, now back to my question again, what is the worst-case scenario?" I asked.

Register a startup

"Well, if we do this and start a company, and things don't work out, then we are looking at a loss of €5,000 at maximum," Maja responded.

I kept thinking about the total number. That didn't look that scary. I mean, I have done riskier things in my life. For example, my first mortgage was €40,000, and I was petrified, as it was my first big loan. So, after that €5,000 was not something to be frightened of.

Before I became a freelancer, I was working for a software development company for three years. So, I had a pretty good credit rating that can accumulate all that debt for this three-month experiment.

And the more I thought about the worst-case scenario, the more acceptable it became. Going a few thousand in debt is not such a disaster.

"OK, so in the worst-case scenario, we do this, and it doesn't work, and we end up with a big debt on our credit card?" I asked.

"Yep, we will owe the bank," Maja replied.

"But then, even if that happens, I can look for a new job and pay off all this outstanding debt in less than 12 months, right?"

"That is a good point. After the three-month trial, we would need less than a year to recover from this experiment," Maja said.

A journey to financial freedom

Looking from this perspective, the worst-case scenario was not that bad. But I had two other scenarios that I wanted to explore.

"And, if the worst-case scenario is that we are €5,000 in debt, everything else sounds better, right? So, for example, a better scenario is to be in debt of €4,000, €3,000, €2,000, €1,000, or break even in three months, right?"

"Yeah, everything is better than being €5,000 in debt."

"Well, what is the best case? What is the other side of the sword?" I asked.

"Ah, the opportunities are infinite," said Maja. "If we prove the concept in the three months, we can continue building the business, further grow the team, and eventually create a huge corporation."

I smiled at the thought of it. I started to imagine owning a corporation. A few years ago, I was at Deloitte headquarters in Amsterdam. They have a massive building with thousands of employees. I kept that memory for some time, as it was a nice thought. Could our business ever get there?

"That would be nice," I said. "And it would mean that we would be financially independent and able to focus more on raising a family."

Maja smiled at the thought as well. "Definitely."

Register a startup

"Well, I have just one question left. Of course, we can decide not to pursue this idea. But how would we feel, throughout our lives, knowing that we could have started but never did? How would we feel knowing that we had an opportunity to grow something big but never had the guts to do it? Can we live with that without eating us from the inside out?" I was gazing at Maja expecting a wise answer. She is full of them, my wife.

"Well, knowing you, you won't be able to continue living with that worm eating you from the inside. Instead, you will get stuck to this moment, always wondering, what if," Maja responded.

And she knew me too well. She knew that as an entrepreneur, it would be a regret that I would carry with me forever.

How many times do we hear someone saying, "I had the same idea a few years back, and now they are making millions out of it?" And how they wish they had done it a few years ago when they had it.

Well, I don't want to live with regrets. I would instead live with the worst-case scenario and accept it. If I was comfortable with losing that €5,000, then everything else is better. And sometimes, the scariest routes lead to the best destinations. Losing a few thousand of euros is nothing in comparison to losing your dream and continuing to live a life in which you are not happy.

A journey to financial freedom

"So, are we really going forward with this?" I asked, my voice edged with a mix of anticipation and fear.

"Of course, once you've set your mind to something, there's no turning back," Maja replied with a reassuring smile.

I was feeling blessed to have Maja next to me. I needed support and someone to push me into taking action. I looked at the worst-case scenario on the notepad again, and I took a deep breath. I was ready to confront the fear behind it. Finally.

***

"Why are you smiling while typing?" Monika asked me.

I shifted focus from my laptop, a bit confused. I got so deep in writing that it took me a second to understand where I was: still in the Vienna airport lounge.

"I am recalling and capturing the story of how I decided to start BizzBee Solutions," I responded. "It brought me some old memories, as I am writing a new book."

"A new book? Already? What is it about?"

I took a short pause and gave Monika the highlights of the book and the chapters I envisioned.

"That is impressive," she said. "And it means I can start directly from the second section, as I am a freelancer and still haven't got the courage to start my business."

"Haha, you will have to wait for me to finish the book, as I am actually covering exactly that."

"Let me leave you to your writing then," Monika said, returning to her own thing.

Sitting in the Vienna lounge, I went right down memory lane. How had I found the courage to start BizzBee Solutions?

PLAN VS. REALITY

I will never forget that road trip to Belgrade, as it gave birth to the BizzBee Solutions idea. The idea was around for some time, but it was on that trip that we made the decision to formalise it.

Once back from Belgrade, Maja and I were aware that we had so many tasks ahead of us. We were both filled with excitement but also with fear. But as I once read somewhere, fear and excitement trigger the same "fight-or-flight" response in the amygdala. We feel the same surge of hormones and emotions whether we are scared or excited. Adrenaline is pumping throughout our bodies, and we feel different sensations like shaking hands, pounding heart, trembling, dizziness, etc. It's not comfortable. So, as human beings, we are wired to either fight these emotions or run away from them. But neither of these responses is beneficial to us. Because when we fight things,

A journey to financial freedom

they tend to grow. And when we run from them, they will keep following us. So, I decided to do the scariest of them. I embraced my fears and decided to do what scared me the most. Start my own company.

I asked my college roommate Martin to help me with the creative aspect – together we figured out the name and the logo. I loved the BizzBee Solutions branding as it suggested "Busy Bees", and it had excellent marketing opportunities.

I could use bees to reflect the social responsibility aspect; the importance of bees in the overall existence of the world.

I bought the domain. I also found a freelancer from Serbia who did our website. It was basic, but we loved it. I also found the office. It was an old 1963 residential building, but with a few tweaks and improvements, it served its purpose.

I even found my starting team of four interns. They were young and eager to learn. And I was so motivated to teach them what I know. Hristina, Monika, Andrej, and Zoran – I can still vividly remember them and, although they are no longer a part of BizzBee, I will never forget them.

1st of March 2016 was our first official work day. We spent the whole of March to get the team set up.

On day one, the interns had to assemble their chairs as their first task. I bought them from IKEA and didn't have

Register a startup

the time to assemble them, but I made it a team-building activity.

Looking back at that time, it was much harder than I expected.

I had to come earlier to the office so that I could plan the activities of the team. During the working hours, I was bombarded with questions from the team. They were young and had quite a lot of questions. And my job was to serve them. Every day from 8am to 4pm. And then, they would leave, so I could focus on marketing and sales activities, as I needed to find new clients and work for the team.

I vividly remember working 12–20 hours daily for the first few months. It was quite a challenge. But luckily, I had my wife's support. She was working hand-in-hand with me, building the business.

We started as a management consulting practice. It was a continuation of my freelance journey, so we offered the same services I had the skills to deliver – market research, business planning, lead generation, and product sourcing.

I have to give you a short background on our services, so you can get a better understanding of my journey. We offered a perfect set of services for entrepreneurs.

When a potential client had a business idea, we would start with the **market research** service to give this idea a jump start. Is there a market opportunity for that idea?

A journey to financial freedom

How big is the business opportunity? Who are the other players in the market?

If we got positive results, our next step would be to create a **business plan**. How will the client capture this business opportunity? How will they monetize it? What kind of marketing, sales, and operations do they need to create a profitable business around this opportunity?

If we could make a solid business plan, that meant that entrepreneurs were good to start a business, and then we could help them both in supply and sales.

Our **product sourcing service** helped them find the right manufacturer for their product. We had good connections with some Chinese manufacturers, and we found one that matched one client's criteria.

From the sales side, our **lead generation** service was helping clients find the right target audience and build a database with their contact information.

Register a startup

Those were our four starting services. At the beginning, my job was to find entrepreneurs with a business idea and guide them through the journey. Sometimes, they already had a running business, so we helped them only with lead generation.

I had one clear goal. I was building BizzBee Solutions to work independently from me so that, at some point, I could take a step back from the business. That was our driving motto for the first few years. So, even with the first four interns, I had clear expectations.

"You have three months to figure out how to continue working without my assistance. You can ask me a million questions during these three months, but that's it. If you can continue working without my help, you are hired. If you can't, you are fired." I have said this several times to ensure that I am setting up the right culture in my company.

And it worked. People were not focused on micro-management but on using their brains to figure things out and solve problems.

A journey to financial freedom

THE CALL THAT CHANGED EVERYTHING

Three months passed. I survived.

And the worst-case scenario – not only that I had worried in vain, but we became quite profitable in the first three months.

I promote two of the interns into a full-time employees, one decided to quit, and one I had to fire. Quite a learning curve for me. But I also hired a few more interns, and in the second round was Nikolina, who grew to be operations manager for several years in BizzBee.

And I was officially a business owner. So, I was able to go on holiday, something that I could not think of for the first three months. I visited my brother in the Netherlands for a week. It was August.

I will never forget it, as it changed my life. As I was screening freelancers' gigs on UpWork, I found a project from Spain that I found relevant. I applied and they asked for a small sample of work – to get an idea of the quality we can deliver.

In short, the project was an AI SaaS that was mapping out the music used across radios, discos, bars, etc. They targeted music studios and artists, offering them detailed reports on where their song was played, how often, and for how long – so they could ask for royalties.

Register a startup

It was quite an exciting business model. And they had an automation tool that automatically identified music with 30–40% accuracy. They needed someone to go through the automation and determine the rest, 60–70%, using various tools and add them to the database, so their system would have 100% accuracy across multiple radios, shows, TV, etc.

A bit of manual work, but as we were not picky at the beginning, it felt like a perfect fit. Maja was able to make a short sample in a few hours, so they could understand better how we work.

And then we had the call of our lives.

"We loved the quality. But unfortunately, we have to scale up pretty quickly. Can you find us ten full-time people for two months, starting a week from now?" the client asked.

I was not ready for this. We were six people in total, and we were already working at 80–90% capacity.

I needed a few hours to respond. I sat with Maja. What shall we do?

An unknown company asked for ten people full-time, and the risks were enormous.

Will they pay?

Can I pull this off in one week? To do so, I would need to find a new office, order new furniture and equipment, hire a new team, and do all this in seven days.

A journey to financial freedom

So, we found ourselves right back where we started. Contemplating the "worst-case scenario". In the worst case, we hire ten people, and within the first few weeks, if we don't get paid, we can relocate them to other projects.

But if it worked, in two months, we would have earned more than we could make in 12 months. The first month's earnings were to cover the office, equipment, and salaries, while the second month was pure profit.

Challenge accepted.

In less than two hours, I emailed a few renting opportunities. I also emailed a furniture guy and ordered desks and chairs. I also emailed our local IT Company and ordered ten sets: computers, monitors, keyboard and mouse, network cables, power cords, etc.

Register a startup

It was pretty easy, as I already had the contacts, and as it was my second office, I already knew what I needed to do. And in my last email, I published a job ad asking ten people to join BizzBee Solutions.

But this time, it was different. We had three well-trained, somewhat experienced employees that could help. They were less than five months in BizzBee Solutions, but two of them, Hristina and Nikolina, had management potential.

Hristina kept the first office as project manager, while Nikolina took the second office with the ten new employees.

They were not ready.

I was not ready.

But then, I don't think we would ever be ready. We did it anyway. It was the right call.

While Hristina and Nikolina were responsible for recruitment, Maja and I sorted out the office, furniture, and equipment installation – all in one week.

And the rest of the team was catching up with their responsibilities. It was an additional workload, but as I trained them, I grew along with them.

And it was worth it. I vividly remember the first day I saw the new office with ten new employees, all eager to learn.

And then it hit me.

A journey to financial freedom

Well, this is a two-month gig. So, what should I do with these people after the two months? Should I just let them all go? And if so, what will happen with the apartment rent and all the equipment I had to buy?

Or should I keep them? But can I ensure enough work for ten people in less than just two months? We were 6 people then, so growing from 6 to 16 is not simple.

This was an important decision. As we were a small business, we did not have enough resources to make mistakes. A wrong decision could mean the end of the business.

However, a new challenge was accepted. It was September, and the project scope was extended to 2.5 months instead of the planned initial two months, so I needed to find work from mid-November for these new employees. And I had no other marketing/sales channel besides the freelance opportunities. That was it. So, I had to work harder: apply for more jobs, do more interviews, and onboard more clients.

And in just two months, I did it. I doubled my sales effort on freelance platforms, offered discounted prices for longer projects, and even took a few riskier projects that I would otherwise not have. But I did manage to find enough work for ten people. Of course, it was not easy, but that's how the business world runs. I was so proud of myself. But I had help. Hristina and Nikolina became operational managers who managed the employees, leaving

Register a startup

me free to focus more on the sales activities and bringing in clients.

Were they good managers? At the beginning, of course not. They had been in BizzBee Solutions for three to six months and had very limited prior experience.

However, they had a fantastic learning curve. They made mistakes, learned from them, and ensured that it would not happen again. Reflecting on this now, I made that our recruitment strategy. We were looking for people who had a good learning curve. We appreciated people not for what they already knew but for what they could learn.

And then it happened again. The same company came back with a new project. This time, it was six people for six months.

Funnily enough, I had already allocated all ten people to different projects. So, I was happy I didn't need to let go of anyone. My initial team had grown to 19 people, I didn't have any spare capacity.

But I didn't want to lose the client, as I saw a long-term opportunity.

So I decided to make another bold move.

You see, once you build up the courage to take the first step, it serves as a catalyst for another one. And then another one, too.

115

A journey to financial freedom

It was January 2017 when I opened the third office: apartment, furniture, equipment, and people. I had done this already and thought it would be a smooth process. But it wasn't.

THE PROBLEM

From April 2016 to January 2017, we grew from one office and four interns to twenty-five-plus employees and three offices.

And I was not ready for this. I could not find work for 25 people. I was overwhelmed.

I was not ready to organise 25-plus people. When we started, I had a simple spreadsheet where I could oversee employees and manage/plan project activities.

With this amount of work and people, a simple spreadsheet could not work. Things were getting increasingly complicated, as I never put any time into developing company's capacity.

And I realised that I no longer knew the people working in BizzBee Solutions when I was doing team building in the past. Some people left, and the project managers found their replacements, so I had no idea who was working for me.

And then it hit me. I am a management consultant. So, I can do an audit of my company. I can review how we do

Register a startup

operations, finances, and economics and audit the entire business.

I didn't like the results. We had chaotic management, jumping from one project to another. We didn't have any employee onboarding in place, so each employee worked differently. But it helped me see the problems and set up a plan for the future.

And within the first year of running BizzBee, in December, Maja became pregnant. We had discussed it, but now it was a reality.

So, I realised that my goal was not to further grow the business in quantity, but that I should start stabilising it. I decided that in the next year or two, I would pause the growth and dedicate myself as a management consultant to improving the quality.

This way, I could slow down a bit and focus on my newly established family.

I committed to focusing on my business original plan – creating a company that could work without me. Obviously, I was far away from getting there.

"Last call for the flight for Armenia."

As I was packing my laptop, I was smiling because this writing process refreshed some of my memories, internal

A journey to financial freedom

thoughts, and excitement at that time. What a roller-coaster.

I had a plan when I started the business. First, I hoped to have a small team and a relaxed working environment.

But then the market intervened and pushed me to 25-plus people in less than 12 months. I know investors look for exponential growth when screening startups, but this was unhealthy growth. It was just building up numbers without ensuring stability within the company.

And yeah, that would be the next chapter – so I should start packing.

Register a startup

KEY TAKEAWAYS

- When making an important decision, plan and be prepared for the worst-case scenario. Because any alternative is better.
- When starting a business, start small. The mistakes are less costly, and it is less risky when you are small.
- As a formal business, you are open to even more and bigger business opportunities, which, as a solo entrepreneur, you wouldn't have access to.
- Exponential growth can also bring more complicated problems.
- Hire people not based on what they already know, but based on their learning curve.
- From day one, make a commitment to build a company that can work and grow without you.

Remember, as a business owner, you are now building an asset. This company asset, if handled properly, can grow and give you a tremendous return in time, making you a step closer to your financial freedom.

5. Grow Your Business

December 2022. Maja was in the ninth month of her second pregnancy, and being a father for the second time was getting real. It had been a while since I had changed diapers, fed and held a newborn. So, I was a bit anxious, but that was exactly what I needed. It was the fuel I lacked to wrap up all unfinished projects and not start anything new. From December, I will dedicate all my time to my family.

A journey to financial freedom

I got back from Armenia. The entrepreneurship workshop was delivered by Joe Kapp, an established entrepreneur and a multi-millionaire. Coincidentally enough, he also grew and sold his company at 38 and retired. The workshop was focused on entrepreneurs, but also how to move from being an entrepreneur to financial independence. Exactly the point of this book, so I was really excited to learn more.

I had the opportunity to discuss these topics with Joe, but as his focus was on mindset and behavioural finance, I will keep that story for another time. I also had the opportunity to network and learn from the rest of the participants.

I also ran my idea about my upcoming book past some of the Macedonian participants in Armenia. They were all excited. For them, it was a movie-potential book covering honest thoughts that nobody talks about. For example, everyone writes about achieving success but rarely covers the internal process, struggles, and all the obstacles that entrepreneurs need to overcome to get there. This feedback encouraged me to continue writing.

Back at BizzBee, the Prospecting and Outreach Summit was also over. And I survived it. These were maybe the most stressful weeks of my life, but the event was a significant step in the growth of the company.

We had to organise the summit from scratch, and we had zero experience with organising such events. In just three

Grow your business

weeks, we gathered twelve speakers from seven countries from around the world in one virtual arena. But somehow the marketing team managed to get it to the finish line. Buba and Tamara did all the heavy lifting, and I just chipped in with some advice; I didn't have an active role up to the actual event.

But even though I did the bare minimum personally, I found it too exhausting. If I just think about the energy it consumed from me, it was too much. However, when I look at it from a BizzBee marketing perspective, it was definitely worth it.

We had so much content generated around it, and we got so many people talking about BizzBee. We put BizzBee on the global map without spending a single cent on paid ads. If we tried to do this with paid ads, it would cost a fortune. But it is not always about the money. It is about recognition and seeing all participants and their excitement in getting the latest sales insights from the summit. That was the greatest motivation that gave us the courage to decide that we're keeping this tradition as an annual thing. Yes, there will be a second, third, and fourth summit in the coming years.

In short, the summit was a great strategy to grow my business. And I think that every company should invest their time and energy into organising such events. Trust me, it is one thing when you participate in an event. It is completely different level of positioning when you are a

A journey to financial freedom

speaker of an event. But ultimately, if you are the organiser, you get the biggest share of credibility. Digital events last forever. As it is recorded, even 10–20 years from now, people will be able to find the event and recordings of it.

And the example of the summit leaves the door open to discuss strategies and tactics for growing your business. I may know a thing or two about that.

My purpose is to share what has worked for me in scaling BizzBee Solutions. On my journey toward financial freedom, this was one of the most challenging steps – creating systems that will generate income for you.

And looking at it now, growing a business is not that complicated. But when I was trying to do it, it did feel daunting. So, let me save you the time and show you how you can grow your business. These concepts are not just from my experience, but also from talking to multiple business owners.

And don't get me wrong. I know a lot of businesses that are simply "recreational businesses". Their founders don't have the intention of putting in a lot of effort. They are simply doing it for fun or some other reason, but it's not their priority to invest in and grow it. And that's OK. I can understand that some business owners don't have the ambition to grow into a corporation. Owning and managing a hobby business is also quite attractive. But that's not why you're here.

124

Grow your business

So, how can you grow your business? I honestly think that most of the first-time business owners have the same struggle. A few people succeed, but not based on a strategy/plan, but rather on luck, and then claim that it was their strategy all along. As a business owner of multiple companies, I can confidently say that the business plan always adjusts to the business environment.

I wish someone just showed up and told us the right route. But that won't happen. Each company is unique and follows its own growth path. I can claim that I grew to three offices in less than twelve months and that it was a strategic decision all along. But it wasn't. A client called me and pushed me to do that.

I can claim that I decided to hire a project manager as a strategy to grow my business. No, I didn't. I had so much pressure from work that I had to put someone in the office for eight hours daily to ensure we had smooth operations.

So, I can humbly and honestly claim that I had completely different plans when I started BizzBee Solutions. I would have grown it as a management consulting business, competing with the big four. But the market feedback threw me in a completely different direction.

From my experience, regardless of how good your product/service is, growing a business means a few things that have to be done right. Without them, you can grow only to a certain stage.

Delegate. Delegate. Delegate

I cannot stress this enough. Learn how to DELEGATE. The first thing that helped me grow my business was the delegation of tasks. I started delegating work to my wife in the beginning and eventually grew into delegating to more people. Like it or not, it's an inevitable step of getting your business to the next stage.

I know that letting go of control feels scary. Trust issues will emerge, and you'll start doubting and calculating your every move. But in the end you'll realise it's a battle you cannot win. You'll have to let go, or you will burn out. Yes, people will disappoint you. But you'll learn to live with that. Eventually, it will all come down to taking that leap of faith. And don't worry. You'll survive.

Like most entrepreneurs, I started as a one-man band. If you are funded by some business angel, you can skip this chapter. But for the rest of us, it is OK to be an entrepreneur and to wear many hats during the day. I needed to represent a whole company with all its departments on my own. And you, too, will have to wear all those hats:

Grow your business

Marketing hat. Yes, I was representing my business. It would have helped if I had spent time spreading the word, building my brand, and creating sales collateral (case studies, social proof, etc.) for my business. As a marketing person, I had to figure out how to make a constant pipeline of leads for my business. You'll have to do all these things, too.

Sales hat. As I was the only one in sales, generating revenue was up to me. From handling the inbound marketing leads to proactively reaching out to potential prospects, I needed to ensure a constant flow of leads. And moving the leads from a prospect to a new client is a science on its own. And you will also need to have a sales hat.

Execution hat. I had a client. Now what? It was up to me to deliver what I had promised. I was the one who was going to spend the agreed hours to ensure the project's success. You, too, will have to do all the legwork, do the hours, drink gallons of coffee and deliver what you've promised to the client. This may be the trickiest and the most exhausting part of the journey. There will be a lot of back-and-forth with the client, multiple people may be involved, and miscommunications tend to happen. You'll have to take a deep breath and count to 100 on many occasions. But, as I said, you'll get thick-skinned with time.

Accounting hat. If I didn't invoice clients, how would they pay? And it was up to me to ensure I would send the invoice and remind them when they "forget" to pay. And

A journey to financial freedom

so be prepared to do these things, too. I see a lot of tech entrepreneurs get discouraged when they understand that it is not just innovation but also plain administrative work to grow a business.

Strategic development hat. I needed to work ON my business rather than IN my business. At the beginning of their business, most entrepreneurs don't have time for strategic development, although if you ask me, it is crucial for survival and growth. Working ON my business means that I need dedicated time to strategize, plan, and think about growing my business. And so do you.

As I started my business, I had to do all this. Whenever I was thinking about corporations, I was jealous, as they have whole teams and managers for each of the topics we've discussed above. They maybe have it easier, but I

Grow your business

had the pleasure of doing something big on my own. For me, it was the only motivation that I needed.

In the beginning, yes, you'll have to do it all yourself. I did it. And I am still alive.

But this is not a long-term concept. Eventually, you'll need to learn to delegate. And if you ask me, it is the hardest entrepreneurial decision you'll ever have to make.

It is petrifying to delegate a project or even a simple task to someone. Will they do it well? Will they consider every aspect? And, the hardest question, could I have done it better?

I knew that I could do a better job than my sales guy. And I had the same feeling with marketing, execution, and the rest of the teams. The majority of business owners have this destructive mindset, believing that they can do a better job than their employees. If you give in to this feeling, it can lead to the end of your business.

So, how can you delegate something you can do better and faster?

One way is to hire inexperienced people and give up expecting that they will do the job as well as you.

When we hire an employee, we evaluate them based on how we would do a task ourselves compared to how they would do it. And, of course, they fail by comparison. We

A journey to financial freedom

forget one crucial thing – they don't share the same level of passion and expertise.

As a business owner, I had to make a mind switch. And it is a simple one. Instead of thinking my new hires were not going to do their job as well as I could, I started measuring my time. If each employee I hired took at least up to two hours of my working time, then I was winning. They were freeing up something every entrepreneur values – time. Yes, you will do it better. But will you have the luxury of doing anything else but work? It's straightforward when you see it like that.

It is how I started valuing the people around me. If they are draining too much time from me, they are not the best fit for BizzBee Solutions. But, on the other hand, if they save three, four or eight hours daily from my time, then they are worth a lot.

I want to give you one last example to make sure you understand the point.

I am good at sales. I could probably close 50% of meetings or 5 out of 10. Probably more, but I don't want to brag. And for these ten meetings and follow-ups, I would need 20 hours in total.

But then I decided to delegate some of the sales calls by hiring a sales manager. And he had a 25% closure rate or 2.5 clients out of 10 on average, and he needed around

Grow your business

the same time as me to achieve these rates. He got better in time, but that was pretty much his average rate.

And here is the magic of delegation. The sales manager is doing a worse job than me, bringing 25% success, compared to my 50%, so I should do the sales myself. But I don't.

As I see it, if I spend 20 hours, I will get 5 clients. If someone else spends 20 hours, he will get 2.5 clients. But in this case, I still have 20 hours free to plan, strategize, and do more significant things.

And, as the sales manager does it full-time, he will eventually reach a point where he will be better than me. It's called experience. And although this example is only for sales, I've witnessed it across the entire company. People are becoming better than me in their own fields.

This is the magic of delegation.

It was similar in marketing. When we started, I was doing the majority of BizzBee's marketing activities. Now, Buba, Tamara and Irena are actually taking care of marketing. And as they are full-time in marketing, they are becoming far better than I can ever be.

The same thing happened in operations. In the beginning, when Natasha took over, she was struggling. However, now I can confidently say that she can help a client better than me. I can strategize all I want, but she has managed

A journey to financial freedom

a few hundred projects, so she has a much better picture of what works and what does not.

Looking at it from a business perspective, I am hiring people to remove tasks from my timeline, giving me freedom to focus on strategic tasks. As we grow and the employees become experts in the field, we can promote our initial team members to managers, so each can manage a team.

That is how I removed all the hats from my head and gave them to the right people. And I believe that everyone else should do it, too. As business owners, we need to focus on growing our business, not micromanaging and putting out fires every single day. For business owners, the most valuable resource is not money. It's time.

Grow your employees, and your business will grow alongside them. Consider it as an investment. Investment in people.

BizzBee would not be what it is today without the contribution of Hristina and Nikolina, the first employees that I promoted to project managers. Without them, I think I would not be here. They freed my time for working on strategy, sales, and marketing. Their learning curve was off the charts.

Hristina and Nikolina were ambitious, and I was aware that, eventually, they would want to pursue a different ca-

Grow your business

reer. But they left a legacy of employees ready for management roles. Natasha rose to the occasion. She joined BizzBee in January 2017 and became our COO.

As we grew, I needed a marketing and a sales manager. As they were working eight hours daily, it added significant value, compared to me juggling with multiple hats at the same time. Dedicated effort beats divided effort every time.

I used my free time to focus on each department separately for a certain amount of time. I took the role of advisor to my managers, giving them guidance whenever they needed it. I was part of the team but the silent partner. I couldn't help but notice how fast things started moving now that I have implemented this management style.

I had successfully overcome the struggle of delegating. It was tough, but it was a mindset switch that I had to do to become a better business owner.

STANDARDISE YOUR BUSINESS

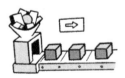

But delegation has its problems – especially in project execution. I had a lot of people working for me, but they were not delivering the expected results. And my clients started complaining.

For me, decisions about what to do in any business situation feel natural. But, somehow, it was not natural for the employees.

And then I realised a simple thing. I had to put all the steps in execution, management, marketing, and sales on paper – so everyone was on the same page. Otherwise, everyone does as they think it is best.

As a business owner, I needed to work on standardisation of all the processes in my business and document it all.

I started with the execution – the most important revenue-generating part. So, first, I created a step-by-step guide on how to serve clients. And that is the easy part. You list all the things that could go wrong and the steps an employee should take in those scenarios.

As I had a team to deliver the service, my job was to ensure the quality of delivery. Sometimes, it required a lot of

Grow your business

back-and-forth with the employees, but I had to ensure ultimate quality.

The same degree of standardisation is required in marketing and sales. So how do we do marketing? How do we attract leads, and through which channels? How do we handle meetings? How do we make proposals?

You might say, we all know how we do things in our business. So why do we need to standardise it? Why should we bother putting it on paper?

I have two very compelling answers.

The first answer lies again in saving time. Saving my time. I had to spend many hours repeating myself when I onboarded a new employee. How we do things in BizzBee Solutions, how to book free days, when we process salaries, etc. For execution, I delivered training on how we work with clients. If it is a marketing or sales employee, I had to spend so much time bringing them up to speed, so they can start doing their job.

Even when I had a management team, I wanted their time to be focused on taking away more responsibilities from me rather than repeating themselves for every new employee.

The second answer lies in the process. As a consultant, I have to map it out if I want to improve something. And

A journey to financial freedom

by mapping out the marketing, sales, and execution processes, I could audit what we do and what we should be doing. Surprisingly, it was quite a big gap, as I thought we were all in sync. So, by standardising the processes, I could start working on their improvement.

It was obvious that the next step is standardisation in management.

I had the opportunity to raise two of my employees into project managers. My strategy was they should focus on operational management while I took care of other things, like strategic partnerships.

We've established six-month plans. I do not believe in three-to-five-year plans, as I am a management consultant, and I can claim that nobody can predict the future in the next three to five years. It is pure imagination and a guessing game, or as we consultants call it – a vision.

So, I focused on six-month plans: what BizzBee Solutions, based on the current knowledge and current state of the market, can plan for the next six months. And the plan would include marketing, sales, service improvement, management, growth, etc. It was a legitimate way of planning a company's growth.

And we still do this. Every June and December, we review our strategy and plan for the next six months.

136

Grow your business

INVEST IN MARKETING AND SALES

The first thing that came up in these strategic sessions was that we needed marketing and sales activities to generate business beyond freelance platforms.

So far, we have been 100% dependent on freelance work, meaning we spent zero on marketing. We were able to provide pricing that was far below the market value, as we had zero additional costs.

But as we decided to grow our business outside freelance platforms, we had to choose.

One option was to keep the freelance channel as a primary sales channel and put all our resources into applying to more job posts and getting more interviews, eventually leading to more projects.

The advantage of this approach was that there were zero marketing and sales efforts. We looked at freelance projects, applied, and would either get the job or not. Simple as that. This way we could guarantee a high-profit margin, as we were in the freelance world.

Another main advantage was that on freelance platforms, prospects were already in the problem- and solution-

A journey to financial freedom

aware stage and were actively looking for someone to solve their problem: that was why they posted the project/job. So, your only job was to convince them that you were the best fit for their job. It doesn't get any simpler than that.

However, there are two main disadvantages of freelance platforms. As you target international markets, you are also competing with global competitors. People from third-world countries are ready to work at a far lower price than you can afford.

Second, the type of clients you attract on freelance platforms can also be a problem. Usually, companies/people come to the platform expecting a lower price than in their local market. So they are quite price-sensitive.

All this is stereotyping. We have found some of our best and most long-term clients on UpWork, but they are a rarity on the platform. But, sometimes, you have to dig the well to get to that one sip of water.

Advertising was never our thing. As a high-ticket service provider, you can't post a Facebook ad and expect people to click on it and swipe their card on a €5,000 service.

On the marketing level, we started creating and sharing thought leadership posts, blog posts, and newsletters. These marketing activities brought in prospects outside of the freelance platforms. This was our inbound effort.

Grow your business

On the outbound side, as we are an outreach agency, we started using our services – we've launched several LinkedIn and email campaigns to start getting the clients we need. And this is how we scaled our business.

***

21 December 2022. It's been almost a month since I last wrote anything in my book. Something that initially was planned to be a seven-day project in Malta back in October is now at a three-month line.

And by now, I have a five-day-old baby at home. My second son, Martin came into the world, and this is his second night at home. I am so excited. Just the idea of having another kid for me was a blessing. Although Martin is my second child, I forgot what it was like taking care of a newborn. It feels like ages have passed since Metodija was a baby.

Without a doubt, I will be staying awake for the coming nights, so it is the perfect time to continue this book. I am fortunate that Martin sleeps through the night, so I can write while I keep an eye on him.

There's no greater motivation in life than being a parent, at least for me. The fact you're responsible for another human being's life will give you the courage and the drive you didn't think you had in you. So, the birth of Martin gave me an even bigger push to get this book over the

A journey to financial freedom

finish line. I don't think many authors talk about balancing the business/personal life.

We all look with admiration at gurus and people who are at the top of their industry/field. However, they need to sacrifice everything and focus only on one thing. And, of course, they will become the best at it, at the cost of everything else.

Think about the most famous singer, sportsperson or businessperson. How much did they have to sacrifice to be where they are? How much time have they missed with their families and friends? Do they have the luxury of enjoying the simple moments in life? Do they have free time?

For me, these simple things were not something I was willing to trade for more zeroes in my bank account. I would rather retire unknown, without a fancy car, without a yacht, but be able to spend a lot of time with my family. I would retire with just enough money to be financially independent. Independent enough, so I don't need to think about paying the bills and putting food on the table.

And this was my vision when I started BizzBee Solutions. From day one, I was focused on growing the business and eventually selling it, ultimately achieving financial freedom.

But not at the cost of sacrificing everything. And reflecting now, this has always been my motto. I want to travel and enjoy time with my family while growing the company.

STRATEGIC DECISIONS FOR GROWTH

The average organic growth is not enough. I mean, some companies grow organically a few per cent a year just by inertia. It is because, as time passes, you have more loyal clients, a better portfolio, and repeat purchases, and by inertia, you grow.

For me, growing BizzBee was a planned and orchestrated process. Our strategic planning sessions every six months ensured that we dedicated time to reflect on what we are doing now, and which strategic steps are next. So, we reflect on the past six months twice a year and plan the next cycle.

It is not that simple, but it is a perfect framework to follow up on where we are with our planned activities for growing BizzBee.

And thanks to these reflections and plans, we made four critical decisions that put the company on the road to success. So, here are the four decisions that turned my life and my business. Decisions that catalysed the growth exponentially.

DECISION #1: SPECIALISED SERVICE

As a business- and data-driven person, I love data. As such, we have data on every client, revenue per client, services delivered, etc. This data has proved to be very useful for future operations and decisions.

Two years after I founded BizzBee, I made the decision to review all the clients we had so far. At that time, we had four services – market research, business plan, product sourcing, and lead generation. Unofficially, there was a fifth service – which is a man for hire. We worked with anyone who could afford us, doing anything they needed. From VA (Virtual Assistance) services, transcription, and data entry – you name it. When you need the money, you do not have a lot of negotiating power.

First, I started reflecting on each of our services.

The first two services, market research and business plans were excellent. As I declare myself as a management consultant, I love them and enjoy helping entrepreneurs with their startup journey.

But strategically, they were not for us. First, it is a one-time service. You work with the client for 1–2 months, we get the job done, they are happy with the results, and

Grow your business

that's it. We go our separate ways till one day, after months or years, they decide they want to make another business idea come to life. It's like being on-call. It's a nice to-start-with service, but it's not a nice to-keep-up-with service. Not in the long run and, especially, not for an agency. If you are running solo, then sure. It's perfect for solopreneurs or freelancers.

And the second and more painful part – it is quite hard to work with entrepreneurs. Imagine a person in their 20s or 30s who gets a fantastic business idea. Then, driven by the excitement, they find a management consultant (me or my company) to help them understand the business opportunity.

As they are excited, they expect a few million euros in the first 12 months. How can you explain to a first-time entrepreneur that things don't work as smoothly? How can you explain that starting a business requires commitment – like working 15 hours a day, sometimes 20, for the first few years till you set things up? I see their excitement fade away in the first few weeks, or they replace it with another "big and shiny" business idea.

Of course, when you are starting a business, you have dreams and expectations. You think your idea is the next big thing and that you're going to be rich, but be realistic. Probably someone else has a similar idea and can execute it better. Maybe the market demand for your idea is not that high at the moment. Maybe you are not willing to

A journey to financial freedom

invest much into marketing your idea. Maybe if you are investing into marketing, but your efforts won't pay off. Maybe the timing is just not right. Many factors come into play.

The other two services – lead generation and product sourcing – were quite the opposite. Product sourcing is when a brand owner hires us to find them a qualified manufacturer (mainly in China) that would be able to meet their production needs. The difference is that product sourcing is on the supply side, while lead generation is on the demand side. With lead generation, we helped our clients reach out to their ideal target and get more leads and appointments.

And these two services were booming. For starters, once you find a client, they need you on a subscription basis, so it is a long-term cooperation. There is a never-ending demand for leads.

You bring a client enough leads, they close them, and the client starts growing, asking for more leads. If you satisfy that need, they grow further, requiring more leads. And we grow together with our clients.

And that is a healthy business to be in. A business where both you and your clients are growing. Even seven years after BizzBee Solutions has been operating, we still have clients who have been with us from the beginning.

Grow your business

From a business owner's perspective, this is the ideal client-agency scenario. This way, you can plan your revenues, recruitment, and you can plan to invest in growing your business. Things that are impossible to predict and plan if you offer one-time services such as market research and business planning.

And this is why we decided to specialise in B2B lead generation and let go of everything unrelated. It was one of the toughest and riskiest decisions we have ever made. Imagine having potential clients reaching out for a business plan, and you are rejecting their money just because you decided to specialise?

Really, really risky. Mainly because you don't know if the specialisation is even going to work. What if there is not enough lead generation work to cover the workload of all your employees? Do you need to reorient the existing business analyst in lead generation or let them go?

But there are, of course, many advantages to this decision.

First, it is refreshing to put a tag on your business. We are a B2B lead generation agency. In the beginning, I was reluctant about putting a tag on my company. Mainly because I was scared that rejecting projects that weren't in the scope of this specialisation would hurt my business. Later on, I realised that not specialising hurts my business far more.

A journey to financial freedom

Before specialisation, BizzBee was a management consulting company. Quite generic, right? As such, we were also offering generic services, like making business plans, market research reports, lead generation, and product sourcing. How generic does that sound?

Specialising in B2B lead generation meant we were experts in a certain field, not just another consulting agency doing everything the market asks for.

We gained clarity and focus.

From a service perspective, as we are now all-in on B2B lead generation, we have the time to add depth to the service. So we've started with database building, added a copywriter, introduced email and LinkedIn services, and many additional services supporting the B2B outreach process.

The clients felt secure, as we specialised in exactly what they needed. If you need brain surgery, would you go to a general surgeon or a neurosurgeon? Even if the neurosurgeon is more expensive?

From a marketing perspective, things improved beyond expectations. When you are a generalist, you don't know exactly what content you should post and what marketing activities you should undertake. It's like walking in the dark; you grab anything that you can hold on to. You have no target audience, so how can you target your marketing efforts? Our website, our social media platforms, and all

Grow your business

the content we produced were messy. They lacked clarity as we lacked specialisation.

After the specialisation, we still didn't use ads, but the content had a purpose. We started creating content about B2B lead generation, and our entire content strategy evolved around it.

We've started attracting SMEs that needed more B2B leads, which proved to be the perfect target.

DECISION #2: SPECIALISED TARGET

Once we had moved to a specialised service, we analysed our clients. As I stated earlier, start-up entrepreneurs are quite a challenging target audience.

I love their excitement about doing things. But when it comes to budget, they always struggle. They have a limited budget, and in most cases, they do the marketing, sales, and accounting themselves. They wear multiple hats and lack focus. They are like me when I first started BizzBee.

We've realised that focusing on SMEs is our sweet spot. SMEs are established businesses – they already have sorted out all the startup problems. They have a client base (clear proof that their solution works), an execution team, an accountant, and sometimes a small marketing/sales team. As they are already profitable, they have only one goal – how to scale?

A journey to financial freedom

SMEs are comfortable investing in growth, whether hiring internal resources or outsourcing to agencies.

I wanted to deeply understand the value we deliver to our clients. I also wanted to know which clients – which kind of SMEs – are better for us.

B2B lead generation for physical products was not our thing. Shipping, logistics, and customs were not our field. We had a few clients, but from the start, it was obvious that it could succeed, but it was not ideal for us.

So, we've further narrowed it to service-based SMEs.

And even within the services segment, I noticed that we delivered the best results to companies that were looking for international clients. Local service providers have to use their local language (especially in Europe) and are more based on personal relationships and physical meetings, so not something we can help with.

And finally, we found our niche in high-ticket services aka the pricey ones. Lower service providers have a lot of alternatives on how to find leads. They can use social media ads, google ads, funnels, etc. They don't need a sales process for a €10, €50, or even €500 worth of service. If a person sees an ad for something they like or need with a tag of €20, they will probably buy it. It is a transactional sale.

148

Grow your business

But for a €5,000, €50,000, €100,000 service – things don't go exactly like that. Nobody will spend €5,000 or more for a service from a paid ad they saw on Facebook.

So we specialised in B2B high-ticket service providers looking for international clients.

99% of our clients were consultants with expensive daily fees or a masterclass or coaching program, digital marketing agencies with annual marketing packages, and tech companies that work in SaaS, Dev, and AI.

We've focused on them. We've updated our website to speak to this target audience. The result was great, and we've improved communication with our clients.

All our written content, like blogs, case studies, testimonials, etc., was around high-ticket service providers.

You need to position yourself as a specialist for your target audience. It is a painful transformation process, but it is worth it.

A journey to financial freedom

Decision #3: Pre-packaged solutions

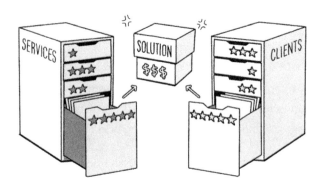

The business metamorphosis doesn't really stop there.

The good thing about specialising in a certain niche is that you can focus your attention on getting to know that niche instead of having to juggle with multiple niches at the same time without a deeper knowledge of what exactly they do.

This goes for the employees, too, not just the business owners. Once they start working with a specific niche, they become experts in handling consulting/marketing/IT requests, and they can anticipate the campaigns' success.

Specialisation has empowered us so much. We know how to optimise clients' LinkedIn profiles according to their

Grow your business

target audience, and we can easily create the outreach message sequence that resonates best with their target audience. This was the magic formula that gave the best results.

We became experts in the field. And as experts, we had to guide our clients on the best route for them.

And eventually, we've standardised these few most common routes over the years.

We made several pre-packaged solutions, which most clients needed, and of course, tailored solutions in case there was some unique scenario we did not cover.

And the pre-packaging process made a significant improvement in our business.

First, it further standardised the work. As we now had packages that clients could choose from, we were able to build templates for those specific services, which led us to be even more efficient.

We became faster at what we did, which, of course, clients loved. Something that initially needed two weeks could now be done in two days.

Also, we've minimised confusion among employees. For example, when we onboard a client, they choose one package – and the employee immediately knows the scope of that package and what needs to be done. Previously, as

A journey to financial freedom

we tailored every service to the client, we had endless meetings explaining the needed activities.

These pre-packaged systems have other advantages. A company offering packages shows you know your customer's needs and have the right solution for them.

The amount of time each package will take to execute is clearly stated, allowing us to experiment, test, and prove great results for the client. This wasn't the case with the tailored services we used to offer. As they were one-off services, the client wasn't obliged to stick with us for a longer period of time. They could leave at any moment. That's the disadvantage of quick wins compared with strategic mid/long-term wins.

We add a planning stage to our pre-packaged solutions when we work closely with the client to plan the outreach campaign. We charge a one-off fee for this, then a monthly retainer to run the campaign.

Previously, we were doing all the planning for free at the beginning just to get a client. And now I realise it was the highest value aspect of the service – the cumulative experience of the management team working with 500-plus clients. So, accidentally, we've added a new service. We have had clients who only bought the planning part and then had their internal sales teams run the campaigns.

Grow your business

In addition, having multiple options gave them clarity about what we do, how we do it, and the time frame within which they can expect delivery.

It is like a mini-project plan – something we couldn't do with the tailored approach, as each project was completely different.

A pre-packaged solution moves you away from the hourly rate and brings you to fixed-price projects.

Both can be good and relevant. But for me, it is a huge difference.

When being paid hourly, my motivation is to be mediocre and deliver the bare minimum results so the project can run, so I can get paid more. The focus is to charge more hours.

Of course, if you know me, I am not that type. But the motivation behind that is to deliver the result while having optimum hours spent.

Paid at a fixed price, I take all the risks. But then the motivation changes. What is the minimum time I need to spend to deliver the results?

And then magic happens. I started to work on my skills even more. I attended courses to be better at what I do. I started to create templates that will help me to be even

153

A journey to financial freedom

more efficient. This way, I started doing things in a different manner, so I could use my time better. I started calculating how I could do something in less time while keeping the same quality of the work delivered.

This was more my way of doing things: constantly re-evaluating myself so that I can provide better quality.

DECISION #4: INCREASED PRICES

Having a pre-packaged solution means you are an expert in the field, and for clients who don't know what to do or what they need, having an expert that helps them plan the campaign is invaluable. They will pay more for that solution.

For us, increasing our prices meant that we could filter out all the time wasters. Even now, I can name only a few clients that paid premium and were the complaining type. The clients who complained the most were the ones we had onboarded at a heavily discounted price.

And our price increase was justified. What we were able to do should not be measured in time.

As experts in a field, you should rarely work hourly because experts need less time to do things. That means that you'll be charging fewer hours but providing maximum quality of work. And it can feel like you are being pun-

Grow your business

ished for being efficient. To spare yourself from that miserable feeling, you should stay focused on solution pricing, as you are motivated to deliver faster results.

I can vividly recall a story about a person with toothache who goes to a dentist. The dentist does a short intervention and asks for a few hundred euros.

The customer, surprised, asks, "Why such a high price? It took you barely five minutes to resolve my pain."

The dentist smiled and responded, "Would you rather have me work a few more hours while you are in pain?"

And this story stayed with me. Clients want a solution for their problems – fast. They don't want a lengthy hourly process.

Over the years I made many other decisions. Some were good, some were horrible. But these four decisions were the most important ones. They helped me position BizzBee as an expert company and helped me serve our clients better. And most importantly, it helped me create the systems I need to keep growing my income.

A journey to financial freedom

KEY TAKEAWAYS

- Learn how to delegate. Letting go of control is scary, but it is a battle you cannot win. Use delegation as a way of preserving your time, so you can focus on the things that matter.
- Understand that employees who work full-time on a task will eventually do a better job than you, putting in one or two hours a day. Growing a strong team can help increase the potential for delegation.
- Standardisation can help you map out your processes, a starting point to measure and improve them. It saves a lot of time in repeating yourself.
- A 6-month strategic plan is a great way to keep track of the progress of your business.
- To further grow your business, you need to pursue other marketing & sales channels beyond freelance platforms.
- Service specialisation can further help in standardisation and focus on your most profitable services. Target specialisation can help you getting clarity in your marketing messages, and attract the right type of clients.
- Pre-packaging your services into solutions will help position your business as an expert, as well as enable you to increase your prices.

Grow your business

Remember, as you are growing your business, you are building systems. You no longer need to manage the business, because you have systems that run the business, bringing you a step closer to your financial freedom.

6. Evolve Into A Consultant

It was **New Year's Eve, 2022**. Having a newborn has its perks. The newborn stage means many sleepless nights that I can use to write and finish this book. Always be looking for the silver lining; that's me.

Maja and I had a system in place for taking care of the kids. Maja had the day shift while I took care of Martin during the night. Luckily, we were blessed with a kid who slept through the night. That meant that I had the luxury

A journey to financial freedom

of free time to get stuff done, while ensuring Maja has a good night's sleep.

During one of the sleepless nights, while I was taking care of Martin, I looked at my New Year's resolutions. I had two main ones for 2023 in my mind.

My first resolution was to finish this book. I wanted to leave a legacy for other people who don't know where to start their entrepreneurial journey. It can be a roadmap for both a potential career and a business with autobiographical elements. I want to be as accurate as possible to get you closer to my journey.

The other resolution was to stop trading my time for money. When you come to a certain age in life, form a family and gain a couple of years of entrepreneurial experience, you start prioritising differently. You realise that money isn't everything. You can always find a way to earn more. But you cannot find a way to get back the time you spent away from your family. So, I had to stop and do some hard thinking. What was exactly what I wanted and needed right now?

For me, it was the freedom of working whenever I wanted, from wherever I wanted. But could I really do this? Will I be able to let go of control and trust that things could run smoothly without me in BizzBee? A concept that, at the age of 35 years, is pretty hard to imagine. It's

Evolve into a consultant

not going to be easy, that's for sure, and I need to do some hard planning.

So, the first thing I did to get closer to my financial freedom was to establish my consulting business and start creating digital assets around it. Digital assets are things that you create once and then keep generating income indefinitely. A book, for example, is created once and generates income indefinitely. It pushed me toward a new direction in my life.

Let me get something clear from the start about consulting. In the 21st century, everyone can be a self-declared consultant. It is not a regulated profession, so regardless of age or expertise, you can "become" a consultant.

And this is something that bothers me. If you haven't spent years mastering the skill or decades in the field, how can you actually advise others? How can you deliver consultancy if you haven't done it yourself for so long that you know absolutely every angle of the skill you mastered?

And as a freelancer, you can also be a consultant.

In this book, a freelancer is a person who is just starting, and freelancing is a way of improving their own skills while working on real projects and being paid for it. On the other hand, a consultant is a key expert who has a proven track record in a certain field and can help you solve a particular problem.

A journey to financial freedom

Let me give you a funny example. I was with Metodija on the beach one day. I bought a fishing rod to have some fun with him. He spent more than 15 minutes teaching me how to fish – confidently, like he had been doing this for years.

He had never tried it before, either. He only watched a cartoon on YouTube about catching fish. But that did not stop him, at five years old, from telling me what to do.

There is a reason why I started this book by defining a skill, and the focus of all the chapters up to here was on further shaping that skill.

Personally, if I was looking to hire a consultant, I would want an expert who has crafted his skill for years and has proven themselves in providing results to similar companies like mine. Not someone who watched a video or listened to a course on the subject.

For me, the motivation to grow in the consulting world was to be able to create consulting frameworks around which I could create digital assets. Now, let me walk you through the process of how I started and grew my consultancy business.

CRAFT A CONSULTING FRAMEWORK

I started my consulting business as a logical next step or an evolution of what we do in the agency.

As we've worked with 500-plus clients in B2B lead generation and appointment settings, we have mastered those skills up to the point of perfection. And we have learned and experienced absolutely every angle there is.

And based on that vast experience, I've started noticing patterns across industries. Although every business is unique, they all somehow follow a similar pattern.

I've started creating our outreach framework based on those patterns. A framework is a proprietary step-by-step conceptual structure that anyone can take and apply to their business. Something that has been tested on many different companies, always yielding the expected results.

Our framework meant different things to different people.

For our employees in the agency, the framework meant outlining the process and steps needed for each step of the service. For new employees, it meant helping them ease their way into BizzBee and having a clear path to follow as they were adjusting to how we did things here.

A journey to financial freedom

For our clients, showing the frameworks meant that they have a clear idea of what to expect, how the process goes, and the timeline for delivering results. And then it becomes a tangible project.

For our sales team, having a proprietary framework meant that they had an asset which differentiated us from the vast competition. As a unique selling point, we would be able to stand out from the crowd.

This is how I created the **ZZ Prospecting & Outreach framework**. It consisted of six steps, each representing a sub-framework of the overall outreach process. Here it is in short:

Step 1: Ideal client profile identification – based on your internal company experience and external marketing trends;

Step 2: Database creation – qualified companies with targeted positions and their contact information;

Step 3: Message sequence creation – a non-pitch, conversation starter sequence;

Step 4: Campaign execution – well-orchestrated LinkedIn & Email outreach;

Step 5: Nurturing leads – response and obstacles handling;

Evolve into a consultant

Step 6: Campaign optimisation – continuing feedback loop and results improvement.

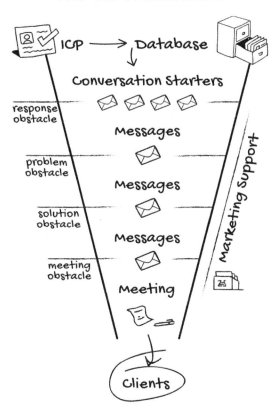

Building your own framework is a lengthy process requiring a lot of iteration.

A journey to financial freedom

You first set up a hypothesis. Then, you test it out on many clients to get some feedback. You adjust the hypothesis and then test it again. And you keep fine-tuning until you have a process that provides the desired results.

Building our frameworks was a truly one-of-a-kind experience. It felt like doing an audit of BizzBee Solutions. I often found that we weren't doing something right. Therefore, I had to work with the team to understand why there was a deviation. So, that meant I sometimes needed to update the framework, or I had to change our process.

Once you have your frameworks polished, it is totally up to you how to make them public.

Having your framework is the foundation of being a good consultant. It proves that you have enough experience working with companies, have identified the key aspects, and have captured them into a framework. And now you are ready to share that framework with the rest of the world.

Having a proprietary framework is a step closer to financial freedom. It is a digital asset that can create passive income. But people need to know about it and about you. This is the reason why you need to consider networking seriously.

Evolve into a consultant

NETWORK

Being a consultant adds a layer of responsibilities to the CEO role. As a CEO, you are responsible for the company's management, and you hold a strategic role. As a consultant, you need to put more focus on networking.

People think that networking is simple. They can't be further from the truth.

I didn't care at all about networking for the first three years at BizzBee Solutions. My primary focus was finding clients, managing the execution, and getting paid.

But when I decided to start growing the company, I realised that I needed to get out there and get acquainted with more people, but even more importantly, these people needed to be acquainted with me. I needed to position myself as a thought leader in B2B lead generation, making my name the first that comes to people's minds when someone talks about B2B sales.

So, I created a task for myself. And I divided it into two areas – building my network locally in Macedonia and building my network internationally.

A journey to financial freedom

Building a local network

To start building my network in Macedonia, the first thing I did was join the local Management Consulting Association (MCA2000). It has around 20–30 management consultants.

Being part of MCA2000 exposed me to the consulting ecosystem in Macedonia. I got answers to some burning questions that had been troubling me for years, for example: who are the key players, what are their expected hourly/daily rates, which companies or organizations pay well, or what are the biggest obstacles we face as consultants?

I was so excited about being part of MCA2000 that I wanted to be more than just a member. So, for the next three years I was a supervisory board member, and then I became president for two more. That was a learning curve. It gave me access to all the projects, activities, and latest information on the consulting activities in Macedonia. As a president, I was exposed to not just consulting activities but also organisations, events, lobbying, and many other insights that I couldn't even dream of knowing before.

Needless to say, I learned a lot. I met consultants with 30-plus years of experience in the field.

Evolve into a consultant

In addition, I joined CEED Macedonia – an organisation that connects entrepreneurs who want to grow as leaders, build their companies, and give back to their community.

Thanks to CEED Macedonia, I connected with many businesses in Macedonia – some of them became clients, some became suppliers. But having an open mind, rather than being just sales focused, was the thing that allowed me to focus on relationship building.

I also joined the supervisory board of Yes Incubator, a startup incubator focused on helping IT entrepreneurs establish and grow their businesses. It was a strategic move, keeping me in the loop of the startup ecosystem in Macedonia.

I also became a judge of several business plan competitions, covering social and creative entrepreneurship and multiple other competitions.

As you can see, networking takes time. As you start building your network you need to be part of the many events, meetings, and seminars that people are organising. You have to talk to a lot of people and go to lunches, dinners, and social gatherings. It can be exhausting, but when you feel tired of it all, just remember why you are doing it. You have to invest time in order to accomplish a bigger goal.

Time is an investment in growing your consulting business, not time wasted.

A journey to financial freedom

BUILDING AN INTERNATIONAL NETWORK

Regarding international networking, I was trying to seize every opportunity that I had.

I started talking on **guest podcasts**. This helped me spread the word about BizzBee Solutions and positioned me as an expert in the field. This opened my consulting opportunities.

Being a podcast guest is relatively easy. All you need to do is search for podcasts relevant to your expertise, reach out to them, and do the podcast recording. Once it is live, you are expected to share the podcast on your social media.

I remember the first podcast meeting that I had. Long story short, I was rejected. The response was that I was not relevant/interesting enough to be on their podcast. That was a hard pill to swallow, but looking at it from the current view, maybe it was the right call.

I kept looking for podcasts where I could try myself out. I did the first 5–10 podcasts in Africa and Asia, where we don't have focus, targeting new and fairly unknown podcasts. I was looking for shows that had a small audience, so even if I embarrassed myself, nobody would know about it. And that was my learning curve – by the 20th podcast, I was ready to go live on air on a US live radio show.

170

Evolve into a consultant

Every time I recorded a new podcast, I grew my network. Some podcast hosts later have been on my podcasts as guests or participated as speakers at my events.

I also joined ICMCI (International Council of Management Consulting Institutes), where I had the opportunity to meet international consultants. That gave me a different perspective on consultancy.

I attended many international webinars, events, and seminars. I learned something new from each of them, and I was growing my network on top of it.

I went to the United States for the first time through the WorldChicago Tech Innovation & Entrepreneurship Fellowship Program. It was my first time in the US. There, I also met 20–30 fellows from the region. We were all part of the Macedonian American Alumni Association (MAAA) and have continued to meet at other events in our region.

Look at your industry and find relevant local and international organisations that you can join. Some require a membership fee, while others are free. However, most of the non-governmental organisations put a lot of emphasis on networking among their members. So, you don't want to miss taking advantage of that.

A journey to financial freedom

Become a thought leader

When I started sharing all the guest podcasting I did and the events I participated in, people started perceiving me differently.

I was no longer just a business owner of a small agency in Macedonia. I was an authoritative person that is well-connected. I became a thought leader in entrepreneurship and B2B sales.

I can't give you the right definition of what a thought leader is. I can only tell you what it means to me. A thought leader is an expert in a particular field, and people follow them and read their content because they know it will help them or their business.

Being a guest on so many podcasts helped shape the stories I tell. Later, I was able to utilise my storytelling skills on podcasts, events, conferences, etc.

As a thought leader, I needed to have my own podcasts that I could use to communicate with my target audience. Even shows where I can start inviting guests.

I produced a lot of content. I started by creating blog posts and newsletters. In the beginning, I was closely involved in the content creation process. Then, I had a marketing team that committed to publishing written content

172

Evolve into a consultant

two times a month. And if you check out the BizzBee Solutions website or subscribe to the newsletter, we still do this.

But I wanted more. Written content is perfect for ranking your website at the top of search engines – that's SEO (Search Engine Optimisation). However, new trends require a different medium. So, we added the audio/video content as well.

I think that I got over-excited, as I made multiple shows, which we are still running. Here are some of them:

Sweet Buzz – I launched this podcast to make it a personal diary, talking for 5–10 minutes about various topics, mainly about how I am growing BizzBee Solutions. It also covers all the challenges, ideas, and plans I have for the company. The goal here was to create a podcast where I could share my ups and downs so other founders could relate to what was happening to me.

I have consistently published two episodes every week since June 2021.

Sweet Leads – a podcast based on the book I wrote about B2B outreach (see the next section). It is a finite series of 10 episodes, where I and the BizzBee team talk about B2B outreach.

The goal was to inspire potential clients considering outreach to call us after listening to the series.

A journey to financial freedom

The B2B Outbound Marketing & Sales Automation Series. I interview marketing/sales automation tool owners on this podcast and discuss how their solutions can help SMEs grow their businesses.

The goal here was to align ourselves with automation tools. We don't intend to enter automation, so partnering with all the automation tools gives us exposure and potential collaborations for partnerships or speaking engagements.

Helping B2B high-ticket service providers grow – one lesson at a time. In this video series, I connect with B2B experts and let them show their expertise, then share the podcast with their audience.

The goal here was to bring potential clients, experts in particular B2B fields, to share their knowledge. A nice lead-generation channel. And hopefully share the podcast with their audience, expanding BizzBee Solutions' brand awareness. As part of the sales process, we can pitch the prospect the opportunity to become a BizzBee Solutions client.

As you can see, I put a lot of effort into publishing and podcasting. In the beginning, it was quite scary, as I'd never done it before. And I am not ashamed to say that I sucked when I started. And you will, probably, too. But cut yourself some slack. You can't expect your first 5–10 episodes to be great. There is a learning curve, and if you are persistent, just as with mastering any other skill, in time you will become better at creating this type of content.

PUBLISH A BOOK

I have never considered myself as an author. Not even now. But as a management consultant, it is my duty to audit what we do at BizzBee Solutions and see how we can improve it.

I would have never done it if I knew how much work it requires to create a book. Unfortunately, I am too busy to dedicate that much time and resources to a book.

But I had a different approach to book writing. It was more by accident rather than planned. The marketing team approached me, asking me to create several thousand words for an e-book as a digital asset. They planned to package the e-book as a PDF and offer it for an exchange of email.

How hard can it be to write 5,000–10,000 words? And that is how I wrote *The SME's Shortcut to Quick Growth*, an e-book outlining the growth strategies we used, market research, and the best outreach to get new clients.

But as I was writing the e-book, it helped me clear my thoughts and expand to a longer content format, an actual book.

A journey to financial freedom

Writing a book would require a lot of time, a luxury that I didn't have. So, I had to find an easier way to do it. This is when I had a Eureka moment. How about I write several e-books that will later become separate chapters of a whole book? It was a win-win situation for me and the marketing team as well. They will have a couple of e-books to increase subscription rates, and we will be able to get early feedback on the topic. And I didn't feel pressured to write as I could create 2–3 e-books and then pause for a few months, and come back to them.

The marketing team loved the idea. I liked it, too, as I didn't feel pressure.

The primary value for me was in the actual writing process. I approached it as an external consultant, auditing the services we do at BizzBee Solutions. And as I was progressing through the book chapters, I realised that some of the things should be done differently at BizzBee Solutions. I had to pause writing the book to improve the processes in the company and then continue writing the book.

Although this took a lot of time to write, it helped BizzBee Solutions offer better services. And it also helped the readers do far better outreach.

Evolve into a consultant

This is how I wrote **Sweet Leads**.[4] The book is about how to identify a cold target audience, engage them in relationships, and bring them to a sales meeting. It became Amazon Best Selling book, making me an Amazon Best Selling Author. And that took a lot of planning and strategizing, but I realised my goal – I was a best-selling author now.

No, this wasn't the ultimate goal. I planned to make it a trilogy – a set of three books covering the entire outreach sales process. So far, at the time of writing, I've published the first, and the next two are on the way.

The second planned book is **Sweet Deals** – how to prepare for the meeting, how to deliver a perfect sales call, how to create an attractive proposal, and all the follow-ups needed in the post-meeting process – everything you need to know to close a new client.

The third planned book from the trilogy is **Sweet Growth** – how to keep the client long-term, exceeding their expectations and ensuring they get the best value.

And this is how my promise to the marketing team evolved into writing a trilogy that will help B2B clients for their entire sales process.

---

[4] Rethink Press 2021

A journey to financial freedom

My second publishing experience was a collaboration project with seven other authors, a book called *8 Qualities For Great Leadership: Critical elements for current and future success*.[5] Yes, the one I mentioned in the introduction that led me to write this book. When each of us contributed a chapter, we had a book of more than 25,000 words, which we could publish in the UK and share the promotion.

Fantastic idea. I don't know why I didn't come up with it. From a business perspective, it is perfect – instead of writing a book yourself, you join forces and write, publish, and promote a book together. It would have ten times better impact and outreach.

Publishing a book was my first experience in passive income. You see, you put a lot of effort into a book, but then you have a digital product. The Kindle (Amazon e-book file format) and the audio version of the book can be sold infinitely, and you collect your passive income. As

---

[5] Yeukai Publishing Services 2023

they are digital products, with simple automation, you can sit back and watch your income grow.

Once you have the frameworks that work, it becomes pretty easy. You can consider different formats.

For example, *Sweet Leads* started as a print book, and soon enough, it was available as a Kindle edition.

We also hired a UK voice-over actor to create an audio-book and target different audiences.

LAUNCH AN ACADEMY

A book, as a format, has its limitations. You are limited to text or audio. You can't utilise richer formats like videos. *Sweet Leads* was 250 pages or three hours of audio, talking about the same framework. And although it included a lot, a rich text format with videos, templates, etc., would perhaps explain the framework better.

This inspired me to consider creating an online academy for the same framework, which could also increase peer-to-peer collaboration.

As a consultant, my first drive was to create a physical academy to train people to become the best at prospecting and outreach.

A journey to financial freedom

However, a physical event would require local clients from Macedonia and a lot of my time to deliver the training.

Creating a digital on-demand academy solved this. I recorded my prospecting and sales wisdom into a couple of videos so that people can listen to/watch them at their own pace.

If you are considering doing an academy around your framework – think twice. It was quite a painful process.

First, I had to do a lot of research to widen my knowledge about how these academies work. It involved reading hundreds of blog posts and listening to podcasts to understand how to do it.

I also had to figure out how to set up cameras and structure the curriculum. I had the book, but transferring the material to an academic format was a technical nightmare. You need to create a curriculum with sections and separate lessons, and for each lesson, you need a lesson plan, what will be the outcome of the lesson, and what tools and examples need to be shared to convey the message. In addition, for each lesson, we needed to consider what templates, tools, or curated resources we could supply to help students in their journey beyond the recorded session.

The recording part was even more problematic. We used three cameras to make a more professional final product.

Evolve into a consultant

One of them was a bird's eye view camera. I put a whiteboard on top of my desk, so whenever I was explaining parts of our framework, I wrote on the whiteboard, and the bird's eye camera captured it.

It took me a while, as the academy was just one of my many activities, so each time I came back to record, I had to recreate everything from the beginning. I put it on pause many times, but giving up on it wasn't an option.

I recall it was 28 and 29 December 2021. While everyone was already in their festive mood, including BizzBee Solutions' employees, I was stuck in our office trying to finish the academy recordings. Together with Gorazd, my lead employee involved in academy creation, we'd spend all-nighters recording as that was the only time I was free.

But on top of the recordings, we also envisioned an online community because people needed to connect and ask questions as they progressed their knowledge.

The final step was to add a live Q&A. I decided to do this twice per week. It was an added value, meaning that you have an expert to answer all your tailored questions and clear up things that you didn't understand from the video lessons.

The academy is a standalone solution, but it adds much value to BizzBee Solutions. Whenever we are now recruiting new employees, the first thing we do is to enrol them into the academy. That way, I guide them through the

A journey to financial freedom

whole training process without spending a minute of my time. They can acquire the basics of the outreach and content creation process by themselves.

So, in my pursuit to become a consultant and digitalise my process, I was able to help BizzBee Solutions simplify its recruitment process. In our job ads for interns and sales development representatives, we have added free access to our prospecting academy as an additional value. It helped us a lot, especially when we were training interns.

But it didn't end there. Having an academy helps BizzBee Solutions to recruit outside Macedonia as the learning and onboarding process is standardised and digitalised.

The academy helped us expand our horizons. Now, in 2023, we have a couple of employees from different parts of the world. We are open to international perspectives and insights since we can all learn from each other to bring the desired quality of work our clients are used to.

BECOME A KEYNOTE SPEAKER

Being a thought leader attracts an audience, so people started asking me to speak at their events.

Speaking at a conference, summit, or event is an entirely different experience from training.

Evolve into a consultant

People you are training make a commitment to listen to you, regardless of whether it is paid or free. You have established credibility as a trainer. Usually people have listened to you elsewhere, read your book, or believed you would add value. At the end of the day, they know you (or know of you) and are willing to invest their time listening to you.

When participating in conferences, summits, or events, you expose yourselves to an external yet mostly unknown audience.

They don't know you – they probably know the organiser or someone else among the speakers. So, the opportunity is to bring new people to your audience. The challenge is to be relevant to them, as they are not familiar with you or your work.

If you have done your thought leadership work, people will reach out to you and ask you to speak, so be ready to make the most of the opportunity.

My first relevant public speaking experience was in Brazil back in 2009, aged 22. Then, with my first marketing agency, AdvertSMS, I got the title of global innovator for 2009 by the World Bank Initiative, inviting me to share my story with the Global Forum of Entrepreneurship and Innovation.

For me, it was an opportunity to visit and explore Brazil. From this point of view, I should have focused more on

A journey to financial freedom

networking, creating new potential clients, and doing a lot of business talks.

But I was 22. So, I focused on learning how to surf and sightseeing while ignoring all the networking events, presentations, and everything else related to the event. I only showed up for my speech – I did a great job in front of 300 people – and that was it.

From a current perspective, Brazil's event was a missed opportunity. But at that time, I could understand my reasoning. I was getting a funded trip to Brazil (and I didn't believe I would get the same chance again in my life), so I focused on exploring as much as possible.

I spent ten days in Brazil. The current Dancho would have spent two months in preparation. My team would have contacted and qualified every participant before booking meetings with me. And I would have spent ten days in meetings, closing deals, and growing the business.

But I was 22, and I did none of that. I enjoyed Brazil's coastline.

I continued my collaboration with The World Bank and had the opportunity to do similar events in India and Finland. However, during these times, I was pretty business-oriented and made many contacts and contracts that eventually helped me grow into a business consultant.

Evolve into a consultant

I have not had a lot of speaking engagements since then. I got into the business sector and rarely had the opportunity to share my experience.

And when Covid-19 hit, everything went digital. I spoke at many digital events, like Skopje Marketing Summit, Global Entrepreneurship Week, etc. But they were all online.

In 2022, I got the opportunity to speak live again. It was the AllWeb Conference in Albania. It was special for me, as it was a physical conference, which I hadn't done for a while. And if you ask me how I did it, I have to be honest and tell you that it did involve some sales and a relationship-building process.

I had built a relationship with the organiser of AllWeb Albania, Darko, who first invited me to his podcast, a show where he talks to media and marketing experts. We had a great one-hour conversation about B2B lead generation. And from there, we kept meeting occasionally. We've been to multiple events together, and at some point, Darko reached out to me with the opportunity to speak at his event.

It was a win. I could share our prospecting story and put my name as a consultant to 300-plus members at the conference.

But it didn't stop there. When the conference finished, the organiser shared it on social media. Then, it was re-shared

A journey to financial freedom

by the speakers and participants, giving me considerable exposure.

And over a short period, I got the opportunity to speak at a lot of other events – Skopje Marketing Summit and Digital Nomad Summit, as well as invitations for mentorship at many events, judging on business plan competitions, and other public events.

For some of them, I was personally invited, which was flattering. But for many, I had to proactively look for speaking engagements. As it was a marketing activity, I had my marketing team take over the prospecting of events.

First, they would screen the world for the most important events that were in my area of expertise – Freelancing, Entrepreneurship, Startup, Sales.

Once events were identified, we reached out to the decision makers, asking if they had filled their speaker slots or if we could apply.

If we got a green light, then we would fill out a usually lengthy application stating why they should give me the opportunity to speak at their event, what value they would get if I were one of their speakers, etc. In short, the team was selling me.

Evolve into a consultant

And then, depending on the topic, my credibility, and the application form – the organiser would decide if I was a good fit for the event.

You can easily replicate the same process to identify relevant events in your area of expertise.

But remember, consider speaking only if you are feeling comfortable about it. If not, don't be stressed that you have to, as I know public speaking is not a strength for a lot of people. And that is OK.

CRAFTING YOUR CONSULTING SERVICES

What is a consulting service?

As I see it, if you know how to solve a specific problem, and people or companies are willing to pay you to solve that problem, you are a consultant. It helps if you can show that you have already solved it for so many other companies.

A journey to financial freedom

If I know how to do LinkedIn Outreach and you don't, I can offer you consultancy on how to do it.

People and companies use consulting services for many different reasons.

One reason is that they do not know how to do something and search for consultants to do it for them. It could be to obtain their recommendations to improve things in the company based on detailed analysis and diagnostics. Or it could be a full service that will involve the actual implementation of recommendations.

The other reason is that they do not have the time or capacity to do something, and they ask consultants to do it for them. It is cheaper than developing their own solution.

A third reason is that they have both the expertise and capacity but need an external independent and objective insight in order to check if their logic holds water or not.

So, there are many reasons a client can reach out to a consultant. The consultant should understand what the real reason behind the engagement is and create a strategy accordingly. When you create your framework, you are an expert in the field, as you were willing and able to put the effort into creating something valuable.

Evolve into a consultant

When you publish a book, you are documenting your framework. You can charge money to show other companies how they can follow the same process or get the same results. And it is a really nice way to differentiate yourself from your competitors.

Looking at my core competencies, my expertise lies in entrepreneurship, start-ups and B2B marketing and sales. I have helped numerous entrepreneurs fine-tune their business ideas and grow them into a business. I work with start-ups to identify growth points and focus all resources on growing the business.

As a consultant, I've learned that quality always comes before quantity. As an agency, my initial focus was to grow in quantity (to have more employees and clients). However, as a consultant, it is usually the quality and the speed of resolving a problem that the clients are interested in.

Plenty of consulting work entitles the consultant to do all the heavy lifting, meaning doing market research to provide recommendations or an analysis of the existing situation.

But if you want to charge more, you must solve a complex problem. The bigger the problem, the more you can charge for solving it.

Imagine you have a prospective company with a problem costing them €1 million in revenue. And you are confident that you have a solution to the problem.

A journey to financial freedom

How much should you charge? An hourly/daily fee or a success fee?

It really depends.

In 2022, I created www.DanchoDimkov.com as an extension to BizzBee Solutions. Its purpose was to separate my consultancy from the company, so people would hire me or BizzBee Solutions.

My secondary goal was to put a price on my name so that whenever a client at BizzBee Solutions requested me, I could refer them to my website. Interestingly, before my consultancy, our clients expected me to be available whenever they needed some additional opinion. This way, I just put a price tag on my advice.

When I wrote the first book and set up the DanchoDimkov.com page, I had to price myself, settling on a fair hourly rate. My goal was to start from somewhere. I knew that as I continued to build my name and authority, I could charge far more in time. By the time you read this book, I hope I will be charging much more than that.

The first consulting client I had was from Macedonia. I truly wanted to help them, so I added a few more hours, as I believed it would help them in shaping their business.

The second was different. It was a UK client with a big problem – his sales process was not converting. So, he

190

Evolve into a consultant

even recorded a video of his sales process before the call. I love it when I have additional data.

So, on the call, I diagnosed his problem and provided a solution. As a result, we've ended up working together further.

My next consulting gig was with a client from Switzerland. The client wanted to utilise the freelance platforms as a sales channel and decided to use a consultant to help them expand their freelance business and bring a lot of new prospects.

It grew from there. I continued working internationally, but I learned one main lesson. I have to be careful with the term consulting since it may mean different things to different people.

When I first started BizzBee Solutions, I was a management consultant, but my approach was different. I would spend days doing market research, business planning, and creating countless word documents. It was a lot of research and typing.

Now, when I founded my new consultancy, I was smarter. I put a limit of 1–2 hours per week as a maximum that a company can hire me for. I don't want to be in a position where the company hires me for 20–40–60 hours, and I am back to being a full-time employee.

A journey to financial freedom

Although my primary focus is BizzBee, I could afford an hour or two per week to help other companies. I also liked it because it enabled me to test my strategies and hypotheses on other companies.

Setting limits on my availability enabled me to be more of a strategic consultant or even coach rather than a business analyst disguised as a consultant.

THE SYNERGY

Interestingly, as I grew into a consultant, BizzBee grew as an agency. We've made a symbiotic collaboration, which proved to be positive for both sides.

As I started talking about my outreach framework, it was also BizzBee's. As I built it within BizzBee, I was testing it on BizzBee clients, and as I couldn't do the execution, clients were soft-pushed to work with BizzBee Solutions.

With my networking activities at national and international events, I was increasing my voice and network. But in parallel, as I was talking to a lot of people, I found many new clients and partners for BizzBee Solutions.

When I published *Sweet Leads*, it was to position myself as an authoritative consultant. But this further helped boost BizzBee's credibility as well, bringing us even more clients.

Evolve into a consultant

When I launched the online academy, it was my way forward in building digital assets, but there were benefits for BizzBee, as I explained above.

Although I was purposely growing myself as a consultant, I was the front face of BizzBee, so wherever I showed up, I was promoting BizzBee.

The more I grew as an individual and a consultant, the more I grew BizzBee along with me as its founder and CEO.

I also benefited from owning an agency. We had multiple occasions when a prospect reached out to BizzBee Solutions needing outreach services. But not everyone had a clear target audience, product-market fit, or even an idea of how to start. Simply, they were not ready for outreach. And I was simply a perfect bridge to help them get clarity and be ready to work with BizzBee Solutions.

There were other cases when a company that already had an established sales team reached out to BizzBee Solutions. They needed more guidance and direction rather than agency-level service. And I was the perfect person to help them set up their sales process.

In these cases, and many more, BizzBee was transferring those leads to me, so as a consultant, I could help them.

And finally, a third aspect was the collaborative projects. We had projects where we joined forces, where I worked

A journey to financial freedom

as a consultant, and BizzBee worked on the B2B appointment setting aspect. And since we are in perfect sync, we could really deliver some great results.

If a company needed a complete Done-For-You (DFY) service, BizzBee Solutions was an ideal match.

If a company needed a Done-With-You (DWY) type of collaboration, I was here to work closely with them and guide them through the process.

And lastly, if a company just needed the knowledge, we had the Do-It-Yourself (DIY) model, where they can buy the book or enrol in the academy and learn how they can do it themselves.

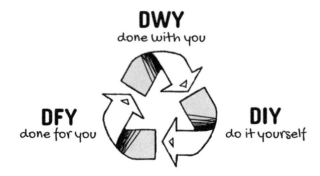

This is how we can satisfy different market segments, all within the B2B sales world.

Evolve into a consultant

KEY TAKEAWAYS

- Digital assets are things that you create once, and they keep generating income, indefinitely. You need to have your own consulting framework around which you will build digital assets.
- You need to get out there and get acquainted with more people, but even more importantly, these people need to be acquainted with you. Position yourself as a thought leader in your industry, making your name the first thing that comes to people's mind when talking about your industry.
- Join local and international organisations that are relevant to your field of expertise.
- Get exposure – show your face (videocasts), your voice (podcasts) and text (blogs). You need to create your own platform, but also you can be a guest on other people's platforms.
- Publishing a book or setting up an online academy is a great authority tool, but more importantly, it is also a digital asset that can generate passive income.

Remember, the reason why consulting is an important part of your journey is to create a symbiotic collaboration between DFY (your business), DWY (your consultancy), and DIY (your digital assets). It is a crucial step toward your passive income and financial freedom.

PART III:

FREEDOM IN SIGHT

7. What Is Financial Freedom For You?

It is **July 2023**. Where have the past six months gone? I've been away from this project for a while, but I have a good excuse.

I enjoyed all the time with my family, especially now that we are a family of four. I don't want to miss a moment of my children growing up.

A journey to financial freedom

We've also been travelling a lot lately. In March, I went to the INVENTO Summit, organised by WorldChicago and Professional Fellows in Croatia. I had a great week of sightseeing and work. In April, I did a retreat in Malta with my friends. From there, I went to Barcelona for the Startup Summit for a week. And from there, we took a 30-day holiday on a Greek island below Athens, Agistri. It is a small, isolated island, ideal for spending time with family on the fantastic Greek coastline. In June, we took another 30-day holiday in Bulgaria to enjoy the Black Sea and all its beauties. And from Bulgaria, we continued to Montenegro, enjoying the Adriatic Sea. All of these were family holidays, taking our four-month baby on a three-month journey. I could finally feel the freedom I was so eager to achieve.

I had many plans with my agency, BizzBee Solutions, and even more plans with my consulting business. However, that summer, my family came first.

I knew that once Metodija started school there would be no more travelling whenever we wanted. Of course, we could use extended bank holidays or winter/summer holidays. But that would be it. And we were used to travelling to Dubai in March and to the Netherlands or Malta in October.

And I started thinking about it. When a child is born, you have maybe 18 summers before they become independent. To be honest, I think this stage happens a lot earlier

200

What is financial freedom for you?

when they are about 11 or 12 years old. As much as I hate the thought of it, I have 11–12 years left before my kids think they are too cool to go on vacation with me.

In the summer of 2023, I knew I had only six summers left with Metodija to be his cool and fun dad. That's why I wanted to use that summer to build the strongest relationship possible with him. And it was a summer to remember.

I think every parent wants to spend time with their kids, but jobs and responsibilities get in the way. And that is why I put a lot of effort into securing financial freedom.

Ah. Financial freedom. Or early retirement. Or freedom to work (or not) when you feel like working (or not) without financial stress.

A topic nobody is comfortable talking about. And I wonder why? Is it because most people are comfortable working 9–5 jobs, and they do it till they are 65 when they can retire? So, it feels taboo to talk about retirement at 35? Or maybe it is because only a few have achieved it, and people are scared to talk about it.

Why is it wrong to retire at 30? Or at 35? Or at 40? Or at any age before actual retirement?

I did try to read about early retirement. But there wasn't a lot to read.

A journey to financial freedom

Yes, there are plenty of books on financial freedom, but all of them are focused on employees. The content is focused on the salary, as a starting point, and then how to start saving a predefined percentage from your salary. Once you have your savings, you can then invest them in various investment mechanisms, and hopefully, by 55, with the magic of compounding, you will be able to retire.

But what about business owners who want to retire early? There isn't much written about business owners. They are different by default.

As business owners, we have the feast and famine – a feast period when we have too much work and too much money, followed by a famine period when we have almost no clients. So, we can't really save a percentage of our salary every month.

As business owners, we think about business investments, growing our main asset, our company, which eventually we can sell and retire. Quite a different approach.

So, before I share my experience on the topic, pause for a second. What does financial freedom mean to you? What is the main motivation that pushes you to be financially free?

I've realised that if you don't know the "why", you can't start thinking about the "how".

For me, financial freedom has three main aspects.

What is financial freedom for you?

The first one is to **live without financial stress**. As a business owner, I have had to worry – a lot. Do we have enough revenue to cover our employees' salaries? Do we have enough to cover the rest of the operational costs?

Only after that can I start looking to see if anything is left for my personal expenses – mortgage, utilities, and food on the table. What if this is a great month, but then the next one is dry – do I have some savings to cover one, two or more dry months?

I constantly had these worries while I was building a company, but as I moved toward financial freedom, they started to disappear. I know that at the beginning of the month, I have enough income to cover my living costs and have more than enough to live a comfortable life. Just waking up with that thought is a huge stress relief.

The second aspect of financial freedom for me was being **closer to my family**. I wanted to be there as my kids grew up. I can work with Metodija to improve his maths skills and be there for Martin's first solid food. I wanted to spend countless nights having long conversations with my wife over a glass of wine or beer. In other words, I wanted to build a bond with my family and create moments and memories that will last forever.

The third aspect of financial freedom was actual **time freedom**. As I don't need to work, I can choose which days I want to work a bit or not at all. Furthermore, I can

A journey to financial freedom

start exploring hobbies that I always wanted to pursue but never had the time to do so.

To give an example, I've become hooked on cooking. I finally have the time to prepare healthy meals for the whole family. My wife loves my new hobby.

Looking at the time freedom, it is quite refreshing to go to the supermarket at 11am, when nobody is there, compared to 4–5pm when everyone is rushing home from work. It is the same with gyms, swimming pools, and other public facilities. The majority of people can use them before or after work. So, being able to visit them during working hours is a blessing that only a few have experienced.

And this includes the **freedom to travel** – a lot. I understand the digital nomad concept, where you travel and work. Still, I like the pure travel concept, where you don't even bring your laptop – waking up on an island without having to check emails.

There is no easy way to get to financial freedom. If it were that easy, everyone would have achieved it by 40 – and then we would lose most of the workforce.

But the more challenging it is to achieve something, the more valuable it becomes.

Let's look at the six-pack body type. Is it easy to achieve it? Of course not. If it were easy, then everyone would

204

have a six-pack. It is challenging and requires long-term commitment, exercise, and a strict food regime. But that is why it is admired – something tough to achieve, and those who did prove it can be done with hard work.

HOW MUCH DO YOU ACTUALLY NEED?

I talked with a lot of people about early retirement and financial freedom. And I always enjoy asking this question, as I can see that people want the idea of early retirement but have no idea what it looks like.

For this chapter, I have a straightforward question – how much money do you need monthly in passive income so you can feel free?

Tricky question, right? But have you ever, ever asked yourself this? If you did, you are one of the few. If you haven't, don't worry. It is a starting point to understanding better where you want to be.

And this question is entirely individual. So, instead of jumping into a number, let's divide it into a few different aspects that will give you a better idea of your number.

A journey to financial freedom

HOW MUCH YOU SPEND AFFECTS HOW MUCH YOU NEED

I don't think I need to explain this. You will need a lot more money if you envision your retirement with a few Lamborghinis, a yacht, and a penthouse in New York. And that is OK. For some people, that is the definition of freedom. It will just be harder to get all that in a shorter time frame so you can retire early.

The alternative is to have an average car, a decent house, and an average standard of living but be able to quit your job 10–20 years earlier than the previous example.

The trade-off is quite clear if you ask me. Everyone wants to have a luxury life and retire early. Maybe a few can even succeed at both.

Luxury retirement and early retirement are two extremes of the same scale. You need to choose where in between lies your balance.

Start by looking at your monthly spending habits. By looking at your previous months, you should know how much money you need each month. But don't stop there.

Is this the amount you need now, and would it be the exact monthly need in the coming 5–10 years? Or is the current living style the one you want to have when you retire?

What is financial freedom for you?

For example, would it include the freedom to travel or send your kids to school?

For me, this was the easier part. As a business owner, I kept some of the business accounting principles in our private budget as well.

We kept a family budget for more than a decade, so I had pretty good data to rely on. For more than ten years, we have kept a daily record of our household costs and divided them into categories like food, utilities, clothing, etc.

Keeping these detailed financial records helps us review our living expenses each month and correct them if needed. We didn't do it to save. But, one way or another, we spend how much we have. By tracking your costs, you can reduce the expenses you don't value and reallocate that money. For example, reducing restaurant meals and migrating that extra money toward more travelling. It helped us a lot, even in evaluating what we value more or less.

And to the current costs, you add the extra costs you need to have a more fulfilling life. For example, when you are financially free, will you be travelling more? Maybe once a month or once a quarter? Local travel or to exotic locations? It adds to the costs.

Whatever number you get for your desired monthly needs – write it down.

WHERE YOU LIVE AFFECTS HOW MUCH YOU NEED

The second aspect of costing is also where you live. Living in the US compared to living in the Philippines can be quite different.

I did a quick research. A single person's average cost per month in the US is €3,189, compared to €500 in the Philippines. That is a substantial monthly difference. And it affects your financial freedom equation.

These two countries I took just as an example. But it would help to consider where you want to live your financially free life. It would surprise you how much faster you can reach it by changing the location.

I always wanted to live near the beach, where there are no extreme temperature differences. As I am from Macedonia, I started exploring our neighbouring countries.

Bulgaria has a similar standard of living to Macedonia, and we can understand the language. However, the Black Sea is not really clean, so it fell through as an option.

Greece has very nice beaches, with crystal clear water. The downside is that we don't understand the language, and putting my kids through school will be pretty hard. And the political conflict between Macedonia and Greece does not help at all.

What is financial freedom for you?

I looked further: Sri Lanka, the Canary Islands, Malta, etc. I enjoyed this process – looking at real estate, understanding the monthly expenses, and the potential problems if we relocated there. It is up to you what you value or don't value in a location.

In the end, we decided to stay in Macedonia. I have opportunities to relocate, but the social life I enjoy in Macedonia is hard to beat.

HOW MUCH DO YOU WANT TO SPEND?

It would be best if you kept the cost equation in balance. Many people keep changing the equation as they climb the corporate ladder or become richer. Initially, their basic needs are renting/owning a living space, regular food, etc. As their salaries increase, so do their costs. It is subtle, but their living standards are rising.

For example, you might switch from cheap cigarettes to more expensive or luxury ones. Or upgrade your clothes and start buying branded pieces. And replace your old car with a brand-new one.

Such costs can easily increase your monthly needs, making you work longer. So try sticking to what you need and value, especially if your goal is to be financially free earlier. My goal is not to work in my 70s just because I want to

A journey to financial freedom

have a mortgage on a huge mansion and several cars in the garage.

THE FORMULA FOR PASSIVE INCOME

So, now you have a number. But that number is how much money you need on a monthly/annual basis so you can live a happy life.

What does it mean? Just knowing your number is not enough. What can you do now or in the future to ensure you have a stable flow of income that matches your costs without having to work? Or how big an investment portfolio do you need, so you have enough passive income to cover your monthly costs without running out of money?

Back in 1994, a financial adviser, Bill Bengen,[6] was looking for a magic number that would help clients to determine how much they could withdraw from their assets each year. And he got to the 4%, which is now the common rule of thumb when it comes to early retirement. Your costs should be 4% of your investments in order not to run out of money.

---

[6] Bengen, William P. (October 1994). "Determining Withdrawal Rates Using Historical Data" (PDF). Journal of Financial Planning: 14–24.

What is financial freedom for you?

Let me show you how you can calculate this. Multiply your monthly costs by 12 in order to get your annual costs. Then multiply the annual costs by 25, and that is the amount of investment you should have to consider yourself financially free. That is the actual 4% that Bill recommends.

Of course, I am not a financial adviser, so the numbers here are recommendations, and you need to see how you can apply or tweak them according to your specific situation or scenario. These are the numbers that work for me.

We will stick with these numbers for the following example.

How much money do you need to have invested so that with a 4% annual return, you can get the cash you need to cover your annual expenses?

Let me give you a simple example that you can easily replicate.

I want to retire with €1,000 every month (passive income). Annually, that is €12,000.

Following the 4% rule, you need to have €300,000 in assets. These €300,000 assets will provide you with an annual income of €12,000 (4%), which, if you look at it monthly, is €1,000 of passive income. Here are a few other examples:

211

A journey to financial freedom

- €1,000 monthly passive income is €300,000 in assets;
- €3,000 monthly passive income is €900,000 in assets;
- €5,000 monthly passive income is €1,500,000 in assets;
- €10,000 monthly passive income is €3,000,000 in assets.

I need quite a lot of assets, right? As this is just a guideline, you can look at different asset classes in order to see what works better for you. Some people buy real estate; others use stocks or investment funds. But that is another topic.

For now, I want you to check your numbers. Of course, if you don't like what you get, you can always go back and tweak the costs in order to get a more achievable number.

I set my sights on €3 million. And 4% of it is €120,000 per year, or I could spend €10,000 per month without affecting my initial assets.

With that monthly income, I could practically live everywhere in the world for as long as I wanted. Want to stay a few months in Paris? I can rent an apartment for a few thousands and use the rest for living costs. New York? I can live on €10,000 per month for quite some time there.

What is financial freedom for you?

At €3 million, I could really be financially free. Can I do it with less? Of course. I can retire with significantly less. In Macedonia, where an average monthly salary is around €500–600 in 2023, I can live comfortably with €2,000–3,000 a month in income. But I didn't want my financial freedom to be tied just to Macedonia, although I've chosen to stay here for now. I wanted to be free – worldwide.

A journey to financial freedom

KEY TAKEAWAYS

- You need to have a strong "why" you want to reach financial freedom. It can be the end of financial stress, closeness to your family, time freedom, travel freedom, etc.
- Find your target for monthly passive income to feel free. Create a personal budget to track your current spending and consider how it will change in the coming years.
- Decide on your desired lifestyle. Luxury retirement and early retirement rarely go together. A more modest lifestyle can significantly decrease the time you need to reach your goal.
- Use the 4% formula to determine the amount of assets you need to have in order to feel free.

Remember, in order to pursue financial freedom, you first have to quantify and know what financial freedom means to you.

8. How To Get There?

Once you identify how much you need monthly and how many assets you need to have to get that passive income, the next step is to figure out how to get there.

When I started BizzBee Solutions at 29, the primary goal was to create a business that would grow in the future as an independent entity that required minimum or no involvement from me. And that was my guiding star for

A journey to financial freedom

seven years – growing an independent company and hiring the right people to keep growing it.

As I was growing the business, there was more and more profit. I returned the majority of the profits to the company to fuel the growth even further.

However, I was allocating a small amount to alternative investment strategies to strengthen my financial independence. But all my efforts were towards becoming financially free. I wanted to have enough investments and assets so that I would be able to live off of them.

I saw five ways to get there. I will go over each of these five strategies and my perception of each.

STRATEGY #1: GROW AND SELL MY AGENCY BUSINESS

The most obvious strategy was to sell my agency, BizzBee Solutions. Even from the initial start, as I grew the business, I aimed to make it attractive to investors.

In 2022, after six years of successfully operating BizzBee Solutions, I hired an external consultant to do a proper valuation. I needed a valuation baseline and a better understanding of the methodology for determining the worth of a business.

How to get there?

It was a fantastic experience, as the questions the consultant asked were eye-opening for me. Questions like: How much does it cost you to acquire a new customer? What is the customer's average lifetime value? How much is the value of all the podcasts, books, courses, and other digital marketing assets? As a business owner, I should have known the answers to these questions. But I didn't.

I had an educated guess on the answers but never sat down to analyse the data and bring it down to a number.

The agency was evaluated at seven figures. I was excited: beyond the financial boost, it was personal validation that all my efforts were not in vain.

But I was not in a rush. I didn't want to sell right after the first valuation. My focus for the coming years was to work the numbers to create a more attractive business. Now that I know how they value the business and which aspects bring more value, I can focus on those.

I started with a reduction of our **customer acquisition costs**. How can we introduce cheaper channels to acquire customers? This kept me and the sales team busy for the rest of the year. But I knew it was important.

Then, I looked at increasing our **customer lifetime value**. How can we increase it? What kind of additional services can we provide to our clients so that they can stay longer? Or how can we improve our services so the client could use more of the same?

A journey to financial freedom

What kind of digital **marketing assets** do we need to build further to increase the valuation of the agency? More podcast shows, more books, more e-books, more blogs? This is one of the reasons why we even started creating new digital assets like our Prospecting & Outreach summit.

And interestingly, although the primary goal was to increase the value of BizzBee Solutions, these questions and activities helped us a lot. Better acquisition channels and bigger customer lifetime value meant more profit. In addition, the digital marketing assets significantly improved BizzBee Solutions' positioning in the market.

Although my focus was to increase the valuation, I've also improved the business. The profitability increased as we improved our key metrics. And with that, I was sure that our valuation would significantly increase.

This strategy was pretty clear – if I can sell the agency for around €3 million, I can invest the money into various assets. And 4% of it is €120,000 per year, or I could spend €10,000 per month without affecting my initial assets.

You know what they say about valuation. It is not a matter of how much you value your business. It is how much someone else is willing to pay for it. So, I needed to find someone willing to pay the price.

How to get there?

STRATEGY #2: DOUBLE DOWN ON DIGITAL PRODUCTS

The second way to get the assets needed for my passive monthly income was to double down on digital products.

I consider digital products as digital real estate. This is because they require a one-time investment (effort in time, resources, and money), and once they are published, they start generating passive income.

Of course, you need to continue promoting the digital products, but if you do it efficiently, it really becomes a passive income.

To use the real estate analogy, I need to make a one-time investment in buying or building the real estate, and then it keeps generating passive income. The difference is that when I rent my real estate I have a physical limitation of one (or several) tenants. I can rent it out, and that is it. I can't rent it to other tenants.

And that is the main advantage of digital real estate. Once built, I can sell it to infinite people. As it is digital, there are no limitations.

For example, selling a million copies of a Kindle e-book for €3 is equal to €3 million in income. Or if I have a subscription service which costs €100 a month, I can sell it to 1,000 people, generating more than a million a year.

A journey to financial freedom

So, in digital real estate, there is infinite sales potential as long as you know how to promote it well.

On the other hand, the main limitation of digital products is that they must be evergreen: frameworks, strategies, and tools that last forever. Otherwise, the digital product will become obsolete in a few years, and you need to either update it or create a new one – which defies the whole purpose of passive income.

And you have to be really smart with the marketing activities, otherwise, you will end up running and managing another business.

For me, there is nothing like waking up in the morning with a Stripe notification that someone bought the e-book or audiobook of *Sweet Leads*. Yet, years after its publication in 2021, I still get this passive income.

And what I really like about this strategy is that I don't need to create just one digital asset and hope it will generate enough income. As in any other investment strategy, I can create multiple digital assets. By having 10, 20 or even 50 digital assets, I am diversifying – some will do badly, some will do fine, and some will sell exceptionally well.

My goal was to cover my monthly expenses from the cumulative income across all digital assets. And by having enough digital products, I can achieve financial freedom. But I have to be careful where I put my focus.

How to get there?

Here are my thoughts on digital real estate:

Book publishing – If I focus on frameworks, strategies, and mindset and not on tactics, the published book should be always evergreen.

With *Sweet Leads*, I focused on the outreach framework and how business owners can utilise it to grow their businesses. Not on tactics. For example, LinkedIn makes a few updates per year. If the focus was where to click, the book would immediately become obsolete.

Also, if you look at this book that I am currently writing, I am focused on strategies and frameworks. I discuss ideas and concepts, not activities. I don't tell people to go to UpWork and click wherever. UpWork might not even exist five to ten years from now. But even more than 50 years from now, you can follow the skill => financial freedom framework, and it will still be relevant.

My goal is to have between five and ten published books, which is an interesting goal for a person who doesn't consider himself an author.

And for each book published, I have multiple income streams: paper books (print-on-demand, so zero effort), e-books, and audiobooks. That's three separate products with separate price tags for one manuscript.

A journey to financial freedom

And by having 5 to 10 published books, I am looking at between 15 and 30 different digital assets, each generating income and contributing to the cumulative revenue.

Books are not just excellent digital real estate. They also help me establish authority and credibility, which directly supports me and my businesses. Each book directs more clients to my agency, BizzBee Solutions, as well as the consulting aspect of the business.

Online academy – If you have published a book, growing it into an online academy should be the logical next step. Especially if you are building a video-on-demand academy. You put a lot of effort into building the curriculum, recording, editing, and publishing, and that is it – you have a new digital real estate.

Even if you don't have a book, you can still create an online academy. If you have any skill that you've spent years perfecting, it is time to share it with the world and show others how they can obtain it.

The academy needs to go a few layers deeper than a book. The book has a page limit, while the academy can be for a few hours or a couple of weeks – depending on the skills you want to teach.

With an academy, you can also offer complementary assets to the book, like templates, scripts, tools, etc., to help your students achieve their results.

How to get there?

The disadvantage is that academies are more how-to-oriented, so the content can quickly become obsolete. So, it might require a few tweaks now and then, but you can keep your academy relevant for a longer period. For me, that is still a passive income, as an occasional few hours of work is acceptable.

I have released the Prospecting & Outreach Academy, and the goal is to create at least five more academies that can continue growing my passive income.

It started as a one-time fixed-price academy. But I've learned that I need continuity and subscription, so I decided to make it a subscription model. I would rather get a smaller monthly income than a one-time payment.

Digital tool or SaaS – Building software is also a great digital asset. Admittedly, it is a bit more expensive and riskier, but the potential is also infinite.

Building SaaS (software as a service) could be quite a big investment as the development costs increase. And SaaS is a business on its own, requiring marketing, sales, and even customer support as people start using it.

However, some micro SaaS/Tools were built ten years ago, and they are still relevant and used. And people still pay for them.

For example, Craigslist was founded in 1995. The current design might have some facelifts, but it is more or less the

A journey to financial freedom

same. And it still gets more than 250 million visits every year.

Another popular way is to create plugins, modules, and extensions to existing famous tools. For example, if you are building a WordPress plugin, you are directly tapping into the database of millions of users. Or creating an add-on for HubSpot or SalesForce gives you access to a specific type of user.

I understand the value of SaaS/Digital tools in achieving financial freedom, but I still haven't run into a relevant SaaS niche that is not overcrowded.

Many **other digital assets** can create a passive monthly income. You can create online communities, evergreen YouTube channels, affiliate blog pages, and many more. The opportunities are endless in the digital world.

But the catch here is that competition is also endless. It is a more risky strategy as there are a billion books, academies, and tools out there, so you need to do your research before getting into it.

My main concern with digital assets is that it is not something you can do overnight. Creating a book or academy takes time. Not days, but actually months or maybe even years. And although it is a one-time effort, it can still be a big investment.

How to get there?

However, there are other routes available. Similar to physical real estate, you can choose to build your apartment, but you can also choose to buy a finished one.

It is the same in digital real estate. You can buy the rights to an existing book, academy, or SaaS and start selling it as your own.

Multiple platforms, such as www.acquire.com, connect buyers and sellers of digital products. In this route, acquiring a digital asset is a pure investment – you buy it, adjust the asset (if needed), and offer it back on the market. This is a perfect route to faster growth: if you want to save time, you invest more money.

Overall, I believe that digital real estate has great potential to generate passive income and bring me closer to my financial freedom.

STRATEGY #3:
PERSONAL STRATEGIES FOR FINANCIAL FREEDOM

I really enjoy the work we do at BizzBee Solutions. So, the majority of my time, resources, and effort are now spent on growing my agency.

But what if the agency fails? Maybe not now, but in a few years? How would I be able to provide for my family? My

A journey to financial freedom

wife and I are both dependent on our salary at BizzBee Solutions to cover our mortgage and living costs.

I've heard many stories of successful entrepreneurs who put a decade of effort into building and growing their businesses, and then, due to unfortunate circumstances, their businesses failed, and they were left with nothing.

I definitely don't want that to be my story, so I keep my eye on alternative strategies for financial freedom. Some of these strategies are quite risky but have the potential to provide a great reward, while others are more traditional and less risky.

I won't get into too much detail. This isn't a book covering all possible investment opportunities and associated risks. There are many books out there that go really deep on this – if you don't know any, start with *Rich Dad, Poor Dad* by Robert Kiyosaki. [7]

I will focus more on my experience with a few of the investments I tried.

Consider investing in real estate – I think this is pretty straightforward. You don't need a formal financial background to understand that the price of real estate always

---

[7] Kiyosaki, R. T. (2017). Rich dad poor dad (2nd ed.). Plata Publishing.

How to get there?

tends to rise. Yes, there are hiccups, but they are more of an exception.

From my perspective, investment in real estate is a quite safe, low-risk investment. In addition, it is a physical investment – something you can see and touch.

When BizzBee Solutions started growing, the real estate question kept popping up. Within the first year, as the team was growing exponentially, I had to rent three offices in three different residential buildings. I was going from one building to another, trying to manage a team. On top of that, I had three landlords whom I had to manage and three offices that needed maintenance. And whenever I wanted to make some office improvements, I was always reminded that I was renting, so there was no point in making structural improvements to the offices.

When we started making some profit, real estate was one of my priority investments. It was the logical next step.

When I bought my first three apartments, I made sure that they were in the same building, on the same floor. This was a relief for all of us, and I was able to bring employees physically and mentally closer. By buying real estate, I immediately had a tenant – my business. And as I owned the offices, I could finally invest in office efficiency and customisation.

Real estate is a common investment of the most financially free people that I know. By renting, you are getting

A journey to financial freedom

passive income. Of course, it is never 100% passive (if you have ever had tenants, you know what I mean). But I would still consider it a passive income, even though, on occasion, it needs your attention. If you want a fully passive income, you can always delegate the operations to a property management company.

The second justification for getting into real estate investment is that, when buying real estate, you have a very nice leverage. You don't need to have 100% of the money to buy the real estate. For example, in Macedonia, a down payment of 20% is enough. And that is a huge benefit. It means that for a €200,000 property, you need only €40,000 as a down payment.

Show me any other investment opportunity where you can enjoy 100% of the asset and pay only 20% to start utilising it. And the 20% is for Macedonia; I've read some surprising data for other countries, where the down payment can be as low as a few percent in total. I even found countries where there is no down payment at all.

And the last justification for me entering the real estate investment is that real estate appreciates over time. It is not just a monthly cash flow that contributes to my financial independence. The apartments also grow their value over time, giving me capital appreciation.

How to get there?

I bought the apartments at the beginning of 2019 and officially moved in mid-2019. The excitement of joint offices did not last for a long time, as in early 2020, we faced COVID-19, which put all of us in quarantine and locked down at home. So here I am, with a significant mortgage and still people working from home. I have to admit – it was a challenging time. If I knew about COVID-19, I would definitely not buy real estate. But it wasn't just me; nobody was prepared for it.

However, looking at this investment decision from the current perspective, in 2023, real estate almost doubled its value in Macedonia in just a few years. This was due to inflation, the energy crisis, iron prices, etc. But doubling your investment in less than five years was amazing. Especially when I didn't even invest 100% of the value that doubled. I invested only 20% but got a double increase on the 100% of the value. Let that sink in. And as the mortgage was for ten years, I am already halfway through it. It was one of my smartest investments. Or maybe the luckiest.

Consider investing in stocks – This is the second most common advice I was given when I was evaluating my investment options. Investing in stocks is actually becoming an owner of another business. Yes, it can be 0.001% ownership of a corporation, but it is still the ownership of a business.

A journey to financial freedom

And as such, it brings its own risks. I got myself into this stock investment world at a later stage. It took me a while to understand the value but believe me, it is there.

As I was financially savvy, I was able to do research and handpick my stocks. I spent multiple hours reading their financial statements, their growth strategies, and their historic achievement. I won't recommend you to do the same – it was too exhaustive, too complicated, and it took me too much time. I did it only because I wanted to learn from the process. As a business owner, you might want to just invest, not learn to become an investment broker. But that was how I started.

My first stock pick was NVIDIA back in 2021. And as I wanted to diversify, I added other layers of stocks – some of the stocks were in the metaverse, others were well-established tech startups like Google and Amazon. But I made my portfolio.

From a current perspective, I got lucky. At the time of writing, NVIDIA grew ~500% in less than three years. But then some of the other stocks I picked failed really badly; Matterport was down 86% at the time of writing. Hopefully, the metaverse will pick up its slack.

But the goal of writing this section is different. It is to find ways to become financially free. An obvious route was to invest in dividend-yielding stocks, so I could start getting

How to get there?

dividends, which eventually would grow to cover my costs. But I took a different route.

I was not ready to invest in stable stocks with stable dividends. My strategy was to invest in high-growing stocks (risky as well) but with zero dividends. My goal was to grow my assets; therefore, my primary focus was on tech stocks. They don't give dividends but have a fantastic growth rate.

Then, at some point, when I see that the asset grows to the desired state, I can sell all my growth stocks and move all the investments to stocks that are focused on dividend payments. At the end of the day, I want to have a stable cash flow. I still believe that at my age, this is a good strategy.

Consider investing in investment funds – This third investment option is for people who think stock investment requires a lot of time in research, analysis, and reviews. Investment funds are the quicker route to investment.

When you don't know which set of stocks you need to invest in, the investment fund should do it for you for a small fee. And they can do it better than you, for sure. They have well-informed and licensed brokers who do investments as a full-time job. So, instead of guessing, leave it to the professionals to manage your investment.

A journey to financial freedom

The value in the investment funds is that they are diversifying the portfolio for you. So, if you chose an S&P500-like fund, it would have a diversification of 500 different companies, so you don't need to listen to the news and adjust your portfolio.

There are different investment funds, so you need to find the one that is right for you. Some funds that specialise in gold, real estate, tech, metaverse-related funds, etc. Instead of buying stocks from just one company, try investing in funds: you are buying into 100-plus companies across different geographies, currencies, and, of course, different levels of risks. If you are a beginner, investment funds are a great starting point. I won't get into more details, as you can quickly research investment funds in your country.

Consider investing in crypto – Crypto is one of the most risky investment options. As a not-yet regulated investment asset, it is high-risk, high-gain.

There are 80,000-plus new millionaires thanks to investment in cryptocurrencies since 2009. [8] That is a lot of millionaires.

A year into COVID-19, in April 2021, I took a two-week Ayurvedic yoga retreat in Sri Lanka. There was a special

---

[8]The Crypto Wealth Report, published by Henley & Partners, September 2023 https://www.henley-global.com/publications/crypto-wealth-report

How to get there?

COVID-19 protocol I had to follow to get there. For those of you who don't know, this is a great opportunity to cleanse yourself.

I met the first crypto millionaire there. He was from Germany, and he was one of the early adopters of Bitcoin and crypto coins in general.

You know, when you see someone glow when they are talking about a topic, you know that they are legit. Even though I had my doubts, I wanted to give it a try.

But I am an economist, so I have to consider risks. Cryptocurrencies are extremely risky and unregulated investment class. My decision was to invest in cryptocurrency only the money that I can afford to lose. More like a gamble. If I lose, it is fine because it won't affect my life. But on the other hand, the gain from crypto had the potential to solve my financial freedom.

To give you an example, I bought a crypto coin in June 2021 and sold it in November 2021. I made a 911% profit on that crypto coin. My only regret was that I did not put all my life savings into it. But then there were other crypto projects that I invested in, and they just went down to zero. A few actually. So, you can't know until it happens.

Real estate investment is safer. Don't gamble the money you can't afford to lose.

A journey to financial freedom

Beyond these few investment options, there are so many others that I don't want to get into. My goal was to show people who are new to investing a few investment options that I had when I was beginning my journey. So, I was not just betting on my company, but I had plans B, C, D, and even all the way up to Z. All of them had a single goal – reaching financial freedom.

My strategy, and everything I did, was to retire early and young. If your strategy is to retire at 50, 55, or 60 years old, then choose strategies that match your goal.

My end goal was to be financially free. And these strategies were just a way to get there.

With enough real estate investment (residential or commercial), I could have enough tenants that would cover my monthly costs. It can be one or a mix of real estate investments, but if you know your end goal, you can experiment until you get the right mix.

Secondly, with a diversified portfolio of dividend-yielding stocks, I could reach financial freedom. Some stocks will grow, and some will fall, but a diversified portfolio will yield a stable monthly income to cover my costs.

And with the crypto investment, I can still hope that it will surprise me with some big financial gain. Like winning the lottery. I wouldn't put money that I cannot afford to lose into crypto, but my hopes are that some of the crypto

How to get there?

coins in my portfolio will explode and make me financially free. I really wish so, but I don't really hold on to it.

Overall, all these personal strategies for investments were great for me. As categories, they all appreciate over time. Real estate rises in value, stocks grow, and crypto as well. If you keep any assets long enough, it can significantly impact your financial freedom.

STRATEGY #4: GROW MY BUSINESS INTO A PASSIVE SALARY

For a long time, I focused on these three strategies above. Growing and selling an agency, building sufficient digital assets to generate passive income, and creating personal investment strategies for financial freedom. Looks pretty comprehensive, right?

At least, that is what I thought. But bear with me on this journey. It started with a skill, but it is definitely not ending here.

Since I started BizzBee Solutions, my primary goal was to grow it as an agency in valuation to a point and then sell it, using the money from the sale to invest in assets that can bring passive income. I think I was pretty clear on my intentions throughout the book.

But somehow, over time and in my personal growth, the primary goal changed. The math somehow didn't add up.

A journey to financial freedom

As much as I wanted to keep my initial plan of selling my agency, the numbers felt odd.

If you are a business owner who is also considering selling your business, let me walk you through my thought process, as it might give you a different perspective. Why do you want to sell your business?

A starting point of the sales process is to understand how much you value your business. Is it a million, €5 million, €50 million? And also, how much do you think you can sell it for?

As an entrepreneur and as a person who spent more than seven years building my business, I have high expectations when it comes to valuation. I started BizzBee from scratch. It was my baby; it was me who put all that sweat and 20-hour working days to grow it to where it is now.

So, of course, I would value it highly as I think every business owner would do.

A better question to ask is how much someone is willing to pay for it rather than how much I value it. Kind of a different answer. I can estimate that it is worth a lot but then sell for far less.

Do you have a number for your business? Are people really willing to pay it, or is it a dream number? Well, let's assume you get an actual offer. Congratulations! I would definitely be excited if I were you.

How to get there?

But then, you have to look at the offer and how it will affect you and your financial freedom. How much is 4% out of that valuation amount?

I can do the calculation pretty easily. Selling my business for €300,000 is around €1,000 monthly passive income. If I am selling my business, I can start earning a passive income. If I sell it for €3 million, it can ensure a €10,000 monthly passive income. Quite a big difference, right?

The key question that I have to ask is – is the offered price enough for my financial freedom? If I sell it too early, I might end up selling it short. If the money doesn't cover my monthly costs, I will need to keep working. I don't want that.

My alternative is to keep the company and keep growing it. Eventually, it will reach a sale price that ensures my financial freedom.

But selling your business is not easy. It is like giving up on something that you worked on all these years. Working late nights and weekends and thinking about your business 24/7. It is a hard pill to swallow.

As I was thinking a lot about this topic, I got a different perspective.

What if I don't sell it?

A journey to financial freedom

A scary thought for me, as since inception, the goal was to grow and sell it. But what if I actually keep the company and put in someone who will operationally manage it? And still, get my 4% monthly?

As I was reflecting on this thought, it became more attractive. It was a refreshing idea.

I was thinking that if (and when) I sell BizzBee Solutions, I would get a lot of money. Maybe a million, maybe €2–€3 million, or even more. It really depends on our financial results. But for the sake of an example, let's say the sales price is €1.5 million.

Here is where it gets crazy. Imagine I sell my company for €1.5 million. Now what?

I want to be financially free, so I will invest the sale proceeds into a diversified portfolio of assets – real estate, stocks, crypto, etc. – with the goal of receiving a sceptical ROI of 4%. That is the plan, right?

But then it hit me. BizzBee is an asset, the same as real estate. I am actually selling an asset that I worked really hard to nurture for seven years, only to replace it with new assets that can bring me a monthly income. What's the point of that?

Isn't it a better strategy to keep my asset but make it more passive rather than selling and just buying other people's

How to get there?

assets? What if I figure out a way for BizzBee to make me financially free?

I will hire a CEO to run the company, and I will still get the same income as if I invested in other assets. If I manage to do this, why would I sell the company in the first place? Why would I sell a profitable company to buy real estate that I need to rent out? I would rather keep the company I've built and get the same monthly income.

I can focus on growing BizzBee Solutions to the point where it will bring me the same income as I would have earned with stocks and real estate.

What a turnaround. After seven years of positioning BizzBee to be saleable, I discover that it is an asset that can provide me with the income I need to retire.

This shift in mindset changed a lot. Why would I sell an asset, which I know inside out, having built every aspect of it, to replace it with another asset that I don't have that strong knowledge of – stocks, real estate?

And on top of that, BizzBee Solutions is an appreciating asset. It has the potential to continue its exponential growth, so by inertia, in 2–3 years, the company can be worth much more.

And the second I thought of keeping BizzBee, I immediately knew who the CEO should be.

239

A journey to financial freedom

I had Natasha, who has been with BizzBee since 2017. Within these five years, she had more operational experience than me, as I was more focused on strategies and concepts, and she was actually working with the team and clients. And she had the potential and ambition to actually take over BizzBee Solutions.

The main problem was, could I step away and make Natasha a CEO? Can she really take over?

It is an internal struggle. How can you give your business, your child, something you worked really hard for over the last seven years to someone else? As an entrepreneur, I vividly remember each setback and success of BizzBee Solutions.

For me, it was the right decision. Why hadn't I thought of this before?

And it is an odd decision, at least for Macedonia. I have never heard of a founder of a small business hiring a CEO and delegating the workload to them rather than selling the company.

But I did it. I knew that I would have to work closely with Natasha at the beginning. Operationally, I was confident that she is the perfect person for the job. However, I knew that my work should be more focused on her mindset and help her grow into the CEO role.

How to get there?

By having Natasha as a CEO, I was finally able to remove myself from operational management. And for the first time, I realised the value of being able to focus on strategic topics rather than extinguishing operational fires.

Natasha took over the recruitment, the happy/unhappy employees' management and complaints. She also took over the client side, managing happy/unhappy clients. And she was good at it.

I was finally able to focus on strategy. And strategy does not have a deadline. So, I was able to choose not to work for a week or two and then do some work. A refreshing lifestyle.

And putting Natasha in place as CEO, rather than selling BizzBee, was also a financial strategy.

I was able to take income from BizzBee beyond my monthly costs. Why would I sell it to buy other assets so I would get the same monthly income? Yes, it is a bit riskier than real estate, but I had the portfolio and the social proof, making it pretty easy to grow the agency.

So, in summary, I got my financial freedom where I wasn't looking for it, from BizzBee. And I didn't need to sell it. I just needed to take myself out of operations. And it worked.

A journey to financial freedom

If I ever decide to sell BizzBee Solutions, it will be for an offer that I cannot refuse. Otherwise, I have already achieved financial freedom.

Don't get me wrong, I am still involved in my agency. I still have an hour's onboarding call with every new client. I still have weekly meetings with the management team. But that is reduced to a few hours per week, and I am happy to keep those. I don't know what else I would do if I wasn't involved at least this much.

STRATEGY #5: MIXING THE STRATEGIES

This last strategy is not a strategy but more a mix of the strategies from above. Why do you have to choose one?

Your ultimate goal is to get to financial freedom. And you might get there through one strategy or a mix.

In your case, digital products may bring you financial independence. Or perhaps you'll go into some stocks or crypto and reach your freedom.

So, how would you know which one is best for you? I don't know either. I recommend a mix of strategies.

What if 100% financial freedom consists of 30% of digital assets, 40% owning a business with a passive salary, and 30% of real estate, stocks, and crypto? Or you can make

How to get there?

your own percentages, but still, a mix of various strategies? Even if each contributes a certain percentage toward your financial freedom, you are still getting there.

Although BizzBee is one of my income streams, I have diversified. I am being paid for my consulting services (still billable hours), but I also have real estate and digital real estate, which keep increasing my passive income. You need to think what the best mix is for you.

The potential for selling BizzBee is still here. And it will always be. Somehow, I kind of love what I do. I am not involved operationally, so my job is purely strategic.

I spent more than a decade in the B2B sales world, so I can talk for eternity on the subject. So, for me to consider selling BizzBee is challenging. I am a serial entrepreneur, so I am always tempted to do it. However, I don't know if this decision will be exciting for me five years from now. Unless I find something else that excites me, I will probably stick to BizzBee.

As a business owner, if you don't have something else that excites you, then what is the point of selling your business?

The mix of strategies worked for me, and I am proud to claim financial freedom or early retirement at the age of 37. I don't care what age you are now; I can almost guarantee that you will reach financial freedom if you take this route.

A journey to financial freedom

KEY TAKEAWAYS

- There are multiple ways how to get to financial freedom.
- If the business valuation is within your desired target, you can sell it. If not, you can grow it to get there. A valuation of your business can show you the metrics you need to work on – CAC, CLV...
- You can reach your financial goal by focusing on your digital assets. Consider them as digital real estate.
- Have a plan B in case your business fails. Depending on your risk tolerance, consider diversifying in assets like real estate, stock, investment funds, crypto, etc.
- Grow your business into passive income. If you have the systems and people in place, your business can cover your monthly targets without selling it.
- There are surely other ways to get to your desired financial target. Or it can be a mix of multiple strategies, each contributing toward your financial freedom.

Remember, there are multiple routes to achieve your financial freedom, each with its own advantages and disadvantages. You need to choose what way works best for you and pursue it.

Done. Now What?

January 2024. Back to where it all started – Malta. I wanted to spend the New Year holidays somewhere warmer than Macedonia. Malta was the perfect choice.

Although I started this book with the intention of writing it in seven days on my previous visit to Malta, I am glad that it lasted this long and that I finally did it.

It took a bit more than 12 months. And the time was necessary. I was often able to get away from the book and

A journey to financial freedom

then return with a fresh perspective and add more value to it.

And, of course, I can wait another 60 years to pass by to enrich it with more life experiences. Maybe if I were writing this book at 95, it would have a more comprehensive ending.

In between, I met with Joe in Armenia, and we have another book in our pipeline – a collaboration that will focus on the next stage. Reaching financial freedom is great, you still won't feel happy without the right mindset. We need to keep growing.

If you do manage to follow the book and get to financial freedom – kudos to you. Welcome to the club.

If you have a way to cover your monthly costs passively, you are ready for the next stage – simply enjoying life. You've earned it.

As business owners, we rarely have time for our family, so now might be the right time to invest some time and energy into it. I know I will.

In addition, I strongly recommend you find a nice hobby – whether you want to start learning how to play the guitar, learn how to cook Italian dishes or travel. Whatever you really like but never have the time to do.

246

Done. Now what?

Reflecting on my journey, I don't think I can completely stop working. I have so much invested in education to stop my story here. However, I will do my best not to be involved operationally. In fact, the freedom is doing whatever you want. This could involve working or something else. Doing the things you love to do is not work; it is a hobby, or you can call it a pleasure. And this is the essence of freedom.

And so should you. I will probably continue the consulting aspect of my business. And I don't mean writing lengthy business plans, research reports, etc. I am more interested in continuing consulting, where I have weekly/monthly meetings with aspiring business owners to help them get to the next stage of their business. Consulting services are not hard work as they are more based on experience and insights we already have. I enjoy these kinds of conversations.

I will definitely continue building my digital products. Whether I will author a few more books or create a few more academies – the goal is clear. Digital products don't have urgent deadlines because we can work at our own pace, and in the end, we have a product that lives forever and provides another passive income stream.

I'll consider being a business angel, investing or being involved in other businesses I like. If I see a struggling business and I know how to help, I can get involved to some degree. It could be a new passive income project.

A journey to financial freedom

Time will tell.

And finally, let's network. We are building a community of entrepreneurs and business owners who are on their journey toward financial freedom. Community where we can exchange ideas and support each other. Just follow this QR Code.

ACKNOWLEDGMENTS

For a book project that should have lasted only seven days, this book quickly grew into a 12-plus-month odyssey. It started and ended in Malta. I am in love with the country. As a small island, it is very peaceful and inspirational.

And I don't regret it, as I have tremendous support to get me going when things get rough and I have doubts.

First of all, hats off to my amazing wife, Maja. Seriously. Thanks for putting up with me – and all your support. In the 12-plus months of the book project, we had a newborn, Martin, who even got to turn a year, a crucial period where both parents (and even grandparents) are needed. And she was patient as this project took longer and longer.

Special thanks to my son, Metodija, for lifting me up all the times when writing put me down. He started school, and although helping him added to my daily chores, I

A journey to financial freedom

loved every second of it. And Martin, although a newborn, could inspire me and bring a smile to my face. Becoming a father made me decide what I wanted out of life and showed me the way to my financial freedom.

I wouldn't be here without the continuous support from my parents. I'm eternally grateful to my father, Metodija, and my mother, Temjana, for making me understand the importance of education. Not all parents would encourage their child's weird and bold business endeavours. You've stimulated the entrepreneur in me since I was a kid. Respect. And my brother, Trajche, for planting the idea of investment and financial freedom in my head, the same as in the movie *Inception*.

A big thanks to my extended bee family. As bees are the most crucial part of the ecosystem, BizzBee's bees are essential to creating this book. Massive thanks to Natasha, Buba, Nikolina, Hristina, and all the other busy bees, current and past. You are the building blocks that contributed to the knowledge and frameworks we've built together.

I wouldn't be as proud as I am of this book if it weren't for all my appreciated beta readers. Buba, Natasha, Gordana, Vlatko, Borjan, Trajche, Igor, Nikolina, Joe and Alex – thank you for your time and effort not only to read my manuscript but also to send detailed comments and feedback.

THE AUTHOR

Dancho Dimkov, MSc Executive MBA CMgr, CMC, is not just a seasoned B2B management consultant and serial entrepreneur; he is an advocate for entrepreneurial growth. With a mission that transcends merely aiding SMEs, Dancho is dedicated to guiding entrepreneurs and business owners towards the realm of financial freedom.

His entrepreneurial spirit shone in early childhood, and at just 22 years old, he was recognised as a "Global Innovator for 2009". This award brought him speaking engagements at major events in different corners of the world, from Finland and India to Brazil and beyond.

He started his career owning a marketing agency, then grew to manage a software company, and he is now the proud owner of the management consultancy BizzBee Solutions. This career journey gave him the experience and tools to make the lives of those particular service providers easier. As the founder and CEO of BizzBee Solutions, he has

A journey to financial freedom

helped over 400 companies, leading to the "40 under 40 award".

But perhaps most notably, as an Amazon Best Selling Author, this is his third book, a testament to his expertise and influence in the entrepreneurial world. His personal life is as fulfilling as his professional endeavours.

Dancho currently lives in Skopje as semi-retired, with his loving wife and adorable two sons. Dancho continues his unwavering mission – to guide business minds towards achieving their goals and unlocking the doors to financial freedom, one entrepreneurial step at a time.

Connect with him at:

DanchoDimkov.com

linkedin.com/in/DancoDimkov

https://linktr.ee/DanchoDimkov

If you want to embark on financial freedom journey yourself but need some help, make sure you check out Dancho's website at www.DanchoDimkov.com or reach out at Contact@DanchoDimkov.com

Printed in Great Britain
by Amazon